T0272547

Praise for *Knowledge Mindfulness*

Dr. Marouf has written a guide for leaders to engage in a personal journey of knowledge mindfulness in this disorienting age of disruption. She orients this path toward personal knowledge maturity—that is less of a destination but rather a process of renewing one's knowledge and ability to take action in the world. It uniquely blends what is personal with what is strategic and practical.

Paul R. Carlile

Professor of Information Systems and Senior Associate Dean for Innovation at Boston University's Questrom School of Business

Adapting to our new normal postpandemic poses a challenge for today's business leaders. Guidance from Professor Marouf arrives at a perfect time to ease you through this transition period and get you on the right path to lead your team to new heights.

Nabil Habayeb

Senior Vice President, GE, President & CEO, GE International Markets at GE

I found *Knowledge Mindfulness* very relevant to any large organization, as successful companies strive to shift knowledge from individuals to "Organization Knowledge" where many can benefit and draw on the vast experiences across the organization. The success of any organization can be tied to employee motivation in engaging with Knowledge Mindfulness and Knowledge Sharing. Good leaders encourage employees to make proper use of their knowledge process and draw on mindfulness to better facilitate Knowledge Creation and Knowledge Sharing. The book directs organizations on how to better build and maintain organizational knowledge and how sharing this knowledge across the organization is an essential part of the success and continuity of any organization. The book addresses a comprehensive model with practical examples and actionable strategies that executives can use to enhance their Knowledge Mindfulness process. With my five decades in executive roles, I found this book to be very relevant to today's volatile world.

Samer Khoury

Chairman at Consolidated Contractors International Company

I found this book unique in its honesty and real-world application. In an effort to be a good leader it is a mindful process of stamina, humility, and the never-ending challenges of things you know and things you need to know in a fast changing world.

Addy Loudiadis

Partner at Goldman Sachs and former CEO of Rothesay Life

There is no better time than the present to embrace the mindful and holistic approach Dr. Laila Marouf prescribes. The only constant is change, and in a fast paced, changing world the golden triangle of Knowledge Mindfulness is indeed an engine for sustainable transformation. As an impact venture capitalist, I'll recommend this book for our portfolio founders and investors alike.

Rama Chakaki

Impact Investor, Partner in TRANSFORM
VC-Co-Founder Mint+Laurel

Knowledge Mindfulness by Prof. Laila Marouf gives the most thoughtful framework for effective leadership. Her detailed and thoughtful approach to the complex interconnections of knowledge, leadership, and organizational success are as insightful as they are practical. With a deep understanding of knowledge management, Dr. Marouf presents strategies that are clear, specific, and on-target in today's business and social climate. This is a must read for anyone ready to be a more conscious leader.

Michael Gontar

CEO of InterVest Capital Partners

If you struggle to understand how knowledge mindfulness can help you and the situations around you, then Prof. Laila Marouf's book is a must read.

Jeroen van der Veer

Former CEO, Phillips

Dr. Laila Marouf offers a model and strategies that give guidance to business leaders for the use of knowledge in more efficient ways to achieve their goals. *Knowledge Mindfulness* sets a path that can help in redefining success and better leadership, whether professionally or personally.

Wafa Ahmed Alqatami

Board Member, Kuwait Chamber of Commerce and Industry

This book is a much needed, timely, and elegantly constructed link between two key concepts: knowledge and mindfulness. As the world hurtles toward an uncertain future, we need to take stock and be aware—personally and as a species—of what it means to be human, about how knowledge enhances our existence, and in the face of AI, how it might not. The heartfelt arc of this book is a real meditation by itself, but the message is very refreshing.

Sanjay Emani Sarma

CEO and President, Asia School of Business;
Professor of Mechanical Engineering, MIT

Knowledge
Mindfulness

The Interconnections That Help Leaders

Knowledge
Mindfulness

Transform Their Business and Life

LAILA MAROUF, PhD

Forbes | Books

Published by Forbes Books, Charleston, South Carolina.
An imprint of Advantage Media Group.

Forbes Books is a registered trademark, and the Forbes Books colophon is a trademark of Forbes Media, LLC.

Printed in the United States of America.

10 9 8 7 6 5 4 3 2 1

ISBN: 979-8-88750-024-9 (Hardcover)
ISBN: 979-8-88750-025-6 (eBook)

Library of Congress Control Number: 2023911161

Cover design by Wesley Strickland.
Layout design by Megan Elger.

This custom publication is intended to provide accurate information and the opinions of the author in regard to the subject matter covered. It is sold with the understanding that the publisher, Forbes Books, is not engaged in rendering legal, financial, or professional services of any kind. If legal advice or other expert assistance is required, the reader is advised to seek the services of a competent professional.

Since 1917, Forbes has remained steadfast in its mission to serve as the defining voice of entrepreneurial capitalism. Forbes Books, launched in 2016 through a partnership with Advantage Media, furthers that aim by helping business and thought leaders bring their stories, passion, and knowledge to the forefront in custom books. Opinions expressed by Forbes Books authors are their own. To be considered for publication, please visit **books.Forbes.com**.

To all leaders—men and women, young and old. Now more than ever, the world needs the full power and potential of your knowledge.

Acknowledgements

Writing a book is always a collaborative effort, and while I'm credited as this book's sole author, the truth of the matter is that many souls have played vital roles in the creation of this work. In fact, every single person I've encountered in my career and my personal life—whether friends or rivals!—has taught me something important, and I'm deeply grateful to all of you.

I'm especially thankful to my husband and life partner, Jawdat, whose constant love and unconditional support made this book possible. Your utter confidence and joyful pride in my work is humbling and made it possible for me to find my own purpose in life. I'm so grateful to have you by my side.

Family has always been incredibly important to me, and I've learned so much from my beloved parents, Yusra and Naif, whose teachings, steadfast love, and remarkable generosity have shaped my own understanding of so many things. My love for reading, my abiding curiosity, and my passion for education all have their roots in their wonderful parenting. I'd also like to thank my brother Nabil—the sibling bond is an incredible lifelong connection, and we've learned so much together and shared so much knowledge along the way.

My beloved children, Fawaz and Yusra, also inspire me and offer me so much every single day. Motherhood is a unique journey, and in trying my best to teach them and elevate my own parenting style, I've learned more—about them, about myself, and about the world around us—than I could have imagined possible.

Finally, I'd like to thank the amazing team at Forbes Books who helped me turn my vision for this book into a reality. Nate Best and Samantha Miller have been utterly calm and capable throughout the entire process, while my remarkable collaborator Ben Whitford worked diligently to unlock my voice and help turn tacit knowledge into explicit knowledge.

Contents

Acknowledgements xi

PART 1:
Different World, Different Needs,
Different Understanding

Introduction 3
A World in Transition

Chapter 1 17
The Need for Knowledge Mindfulness

PART 2:
Zooming In: The Elements of
Knowledge Mindfulness

Chapter 2 47
Understanding Knowledge

Chapter 3 79
Understanding Self

Chapter 4 103
Understanding the External World

PART 3:
Zooming Out: The Moving Engine
of Knowledge Mindfulness

Chapter 5 125
The Path to Knowledge Maturity

Chapter 6 137
Create (yet Keep Renewing)

Chapter 7 155
Connect (yet Keep Disconnecting)

Chapter 8 175
Capitalize (yet Keep Acting)

Conclusion 197
Make Your Life Worth Living

Endnotes. 213

Part 1:

Different World,
Different Needs,
Different Understanding

A World in Transition

S ometimes you have to step back in order to leap forward. In early 2020 I stepped away. I'd spent many years as an academic, authoring scores of research articles exploring the diverse ways in which organizations generate, share, and use knowledge. I'd begun my career studying computer science, then completed a PhD in information science with a focus on knowledge management, going on to become a professor, researcher, and consultant. Along the way I'd become a leader in my university, too, supporting my colleagues as they translated theories into real-world innovations, patented and commercialized their novel ideas, and brought their breakthroughs to a wider audience.

It was rewarding work—but after years of service, I needed to refocus and recharge. My employer, Kuwait University, awarded me a two-year sabbatical, starting with a few months working at the Massachusetts Institute of Technology's Open Learning Center alongside some of the most respected minds in learning and innovation. When I boarded my flight to Boston, I was eagerly anticipating an energizing, and perhaps even career-defining, opportunity to reflect on the journey I'd taken and dig deeper into the problems that fascinated me.

Of course, the world had other plans.

Almost as soon as my plane landed, the COVID-19 pandemic began. Overnight, the MIT campus closed down. So did the airlines. All those world-leading experts canceled their classes and headed off to their country homes. Along with my husband and our two children, I was stuck, far from home, wandering the chilly and suddenly deserted streets of Boston.

An Unexpected Gift

I didn't realize it right away, but the interruption of my planned sabbatical was the best thing that could possibly have happened to me. With nobody to talk to, and no libraries to hide away in, I had the time and mental space to reflect and ask myself some tough questions. "What if things never go back to normal?" I wondered. "Everything's changed—so what do I want to do next?"

Forget the intellectual and professional momentum I'd built up and the academic theories I'd assumed I'd spend the next year thinking about. Forced to look inward, I realized I'd gotten stuck in a groove. I'd spent my life studying knowledge but never asked what all my own knowledge added up to.

Record scratch! Stranded in Boston, I found myself stepping back and asking—for the first time in years—what really mattered to me. Would my knowledge help me to achieve those goals? In what ways? And how could I work to accelerate and guide that process?

This book is the result of that stocktaking. When I looked in the mirror, I found myself asking not just how I could do my job better, but whether I should continue in the same path I was on. I loved studying and teaching, but the more I reflected, the more I felt it was time to move beyond the narrow hallways of academia. Academic research is necessarily fragmented into specialized fields and subfields. I wanted to zoom out and let the world be my classroom—to write a new syllabus for myself and others that focused not on narrow specializations, but on the intersections and interstitial spaces that lie *between* disciplines.

I loved my organization—the department I called home, the university I served,

> *I'd spent my life studying knowledge but never asked what all my own knowledge added up to.*

and the broader academic community of which I was part. But as I looked back on my work, I came to see that the siloed nature of academia had constrained not only my teaching and research, but also the way I related to knowledge itself.

Knowledge, of course, is an intensely personal thing. As Peter Drucker notes, knowledge is "embodied in a person; carried by a person; created, augmented or improved by a person; applied by a person … [and] used or misused by a person."[1] During my years studying knowledge management, I'd seen the individual recentered as the basic unit of organizational knowledge, with "personal knowledge management" introduced as a kind of bottom-up addition to conventional knowledge management theories. The better we equipped individual workers to deal with knowledge, the theory went, the more knowledge and innovation they would unlock for their organizations.

But as Drucker also writes, knowledge itself is changing fast. "It is the nature of knowledge," Drucker says, "that it changes fast and that today's certainties always become tomorrow's absurdities."[2] I couldn't help but feel that the fragmented and slow-moving bureaucracy of academia was ill equipped to cope with the new kinds of knowledge we need in today's fast-changing world.

A New Perspective on Knowledge and Knowledge Management

The quest to understand and unlock that knowledge dates back thousands of years, across the entire course of human history. The focus of that quest keeps changing, though, as times and people's needs change. I had focused for many years on organizational knowledge in my teachings and research, but I had been too zoomed in to meaningfully engage with all those *other* ways of thinking about knowledge. It was only when I stopped and stepped away that new possibilities appeared to me.

An organization's knowledge, I realized, is not only an intangible asset, like cash on a balance sheet, but also something much more powerful and dynamic—a living system woven from the rich and varied inner lives and collective human wisdom of interconnected groups of countless diverse individuals.

Back when I started my PhD, people thought of knowledge as primarily a process of onboarding and digesting knowledge from the outside world, like a computer operating on inputs and producing outputs. As we'll see, that approach has some serious limitations, but it's a prevalent view that's worth understanding clearly.

In this conception, shown in the chart below, the right-hand circle represents our tacit knowledge. This is the "content" of our thinking; it's the sum of all our varied experiences, skills like riding a bike or speaking a language, and all the things that exist in our head through the action of our rational mind.

The left-hand circle, on the other hand, represents the outside world. Obviously, a huge amount of knowledge exists in the world in the form of data and information, but it has limited meaning to me until it's processed by my rational mind. For simplicity's sake we refer to this as explicit knowledge, but it encompasses anything outside ourselves that hasn't yet made it into our heads: books and essays and podcasts, the things experts and teachers convey through lessons or conversations, raw data that others have distilled into structured information, and more.

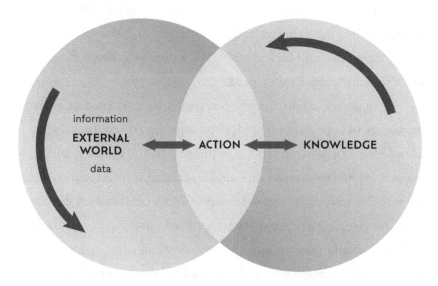

These two circles are constantly churning and changing, so there's plenty of movement between external and internal knowledge. This nexus between the two is where much of what matters most happens—it's where we bring together information and experience, where the world around us shapes and adds to our stock of knowledge, and where we use our own thoughts, unique knowledge, and insights to shape the world around us.

The boundaries between these two circles are permeable, and in an ideal world, exchanges and interactions between these two domains—between the world and our knowledge—would take place in a fairly orderly, or at least manageable and coherent, way, like a computer processing inputs and spitting out analyses.

That's the goal of the discipline of knowledge management—a field that reflects organizations' increasing recognition that tacit knowledge can be a vital source of competitive advantage. New technologies have made explicit knowledge and information increasingly abundant in our professional lives, but since the early 1990s, organizations have begun to understand the necessity of *also* leveraging tacit knowledge—the stuff locked away inside their employees' heads—in order to get the results they need.

Virtually most Fortune 500 companies have adopted knowledge management approaches that focus on capturing or externalizing tacit knowledge—by writing reports, taping Q and A sessions, conducting exit interviews, and so on—and inscribing it into organizational memory by recording it in databases or other information depositories. The goal, in such approaches, has been efficiency: organizations seek to translate one employee's tacit knowledge into a format that allows it to be quickly accessed and used by another employee.

Unfortunately, most such efforts have fallen short. Organizations have slowly begun to realize that tacit knowledge is *personal*. It can't simply be extracted from the employee's head and converted into explicit knowledge, because much of its value comes from the context, the cues, and the meaning it holds for the individual employee.

To try to overcome this, organizations have tried other approaches such as creating communities of practice: instead of attempting to extract and capture knowledge, these methods encourage and empower employees to share their tacit knowledge with others. This approach has proven valuable and is still used successfully today.

Such efforts have given rise to new branches of knowledge management—"personal knowledge management"—that focus on leveraging an individual's tacit knowledge to create value for the individual themselves. Such approaches haven't found much traction in organizations, though, perhaps because they fail to connect the individual benefits they deliver with organizational value.

So you might ask, how is it then that knowledge and knowledge management can help us find a path forward through a world in transition? The reality is that our changing world *demands* a new way of understanding: a more complex form of knowledge capable of dealing with the complexities of a world in flux. We have been left adrift, anchorless, and in need of a new understanding and a new approach.

A New Approach

Instead of poring over the latest research articles that were being published to find a new approach, I began looking elsewhere. Over the next few months, I took online classes on leadership at Columbia University, on design thinking at Stanford University, and on entrepreneurship at Babson College. I found that the most enriching parts of these programs were the virtual communities and informal discussions that sprang up around them. Seeking similar connections, I also joined Abundance Digital, a membership program founded by Peter

Diamandis to provide access to tech breakthroughs and disruptive business innovations.

It was there that I was introduced—via an AI-powered match-making service, no less!—to Ode, a nurse from south Florida who loved her work as a caregiver but had started to feel that medical science couldn't capture the whole story about what it meant to be human. We started meeting up on Zoom every week or so—first to discuss new technologies, psychology, business, and other topics and later simply to talk about our lives.

Ode opened my eyes in many ways. We had what sociologist Mark Granovetter famously described as a "weak tie"—we weren't family or incredibly close friends, but precisely because we didn't come from the exact same circles, we were able to awaken one another to new perspectives and ways of thinking.[3] We spoke for hours about our struggles during the COVID crisis and—especially following the death of George Floyd—about our experiences as people of color. I admired Ode's clarity of purpose and her ability to step away from ways of knowing that no longer served her goals. Fascinated by spiritual aspects of African dance, Ode had begun to question the connection between mind and body—and finding herself asking questions that medical science couldn't answer, she broke loose from her organizational ties and sought new answers.

Today, Ode and her family are living in Africa, where Ode is continuing her journey and exploring non-Western ideas about mind and body. I didn't necessarily feel the same way as Ode about the importance of African dance. (If I did, I'd be dancing instead of writing this book.) But I deeply admire her conviction—her willingness to assess what she knew, diagnose what was lacking, and move decisively in bold new directions.

Ode's story inspired me. I found myself turning away from the patterns of thinking I'd previously known and envisioning a new path forward. I felt ready to rewire and to commit my time, energy, and resources to the adventure to which I'd been drawn. I grew more methodological and purposeful about reshaping my understanding of knowledge and knowledge management—from one anchored in the old world order to a new conceptual model that I sensed would be better suited to the emerging postpandemic world.

I call that new framework Knowledge Mindfulness, and it reflects a reframing of knowledge management to encompass not just individuals as nodes within networks of knowledge, but also the recognition that individuals are *themselves* networks—multifaceted human beings made up of many different desires, goals, values, beliefs, and unique perspectives and themselves deeply interconnected with many other systems and networks.

Seen through this lens, the organization emerges as a complex living system made up of countless *other* complex living systems. To lead organizations effectively, then, we need to recenter the individual, conceived holistically, and to work to understand all the hidden connections within which each individual is embedded. Only by understanding these interconnections, and all the pressures and possibilities that come with being an individual in a world in transition, I'll suggest, can we drive both individuals and organizations forward and develop adaptable, purposeful, and compassionate ways of thinking and being in a chaotic and ever-changing world.

That's necessary because in a transitional world, by definition, things are out of balance. The outside world has begun to cycle faster and faster, expanding and evolving because of the expansion of explicit knowledge. Bombarded by ever-increasing volumes of data and information, we find ourselves immersed in complexity and ambiguity that no one person could possibly understand or make sense of. The movement between external and internal, and our ability to cycle knowledge through that precious nexus to turn it into purposeful action, begins to wane almost to nothing.

In the next chapter, I'll ask you to consider the ways in which the world we share is volatile, uncertain, changing, and ambiguous, or what military leaders call VUCA. Our world has always been pretty unstable, but today—in the grips of technological transformation, a pandemic, social upheaval, and more—the old ways of thinking about and understanding knowledge are simply unsustainable.

In a VUCA world, we live in the grips of uncertainty and instability. All too often that leaves us unhappy, unproductive, paralyzed by a surfeit of information and a lack of clarity. That's bad for individuals and terrible for organizations, too—because when individuals lack insight, wisdom, and coherency, they can't serve themselves, their organizations, or each other in effective ways. We need a fresh approach, and—spoiler alert!—I believe that Knowledge Mindfulness is the new paradigm today's leaders need.

The second part of the book zooms in to lay out the conceptual foundations of Knowledge Mindfulness and show the interconnections between knowledge, self, and the external world. In addition we will show why knowledge mindfulness is important for leaders and the impact they will have if they start using this approach. By exploring these elements individually, we'll surface multidimensional complexities to which most of us probably haven't previously paid much attention.

First, we'll explore a new perspective on knowledge. Knowledge, we'll learn, is much more holistic and human than is often believed:

intuition, not just reasoning, plays a vital role by providing us with direct experiences that supplement or supplant the sensory data and information upon which we would otherwise have to rely. Crucially, we'll come to recognize how knowledge emerges from the interplay between the internal and external world and serves as a bridge between the two.

Second, with that foundation we'll move on to consider the ways in which knowledge depends on inward reflection and on arriving at a deep understanding of ourselves. Knowledge Mindfulness, I'll argue, is hard to attain if we aren't willing to ask tough questions about what we know and don't know and why we need to know certain things— and also to probe the ways in which our personality, our preferences, and our biases impact the things we pay attention to and the kinds of information we draw inward and use. We'll learn how to integrate knowledge into our understanding of ourselves—and also how to use that understanding to strengthen our presence in our organization and build deeper connections with our employees.

Third, we'll explore the way that our knowledge is context dependent and the way that our ecosystem of social connections both shapes and is shaped by our knowledge. Thinking about knowledge might seem inherently insular, but I'll argue that Knowledge Mindfulness can only come when we commit to looking outward and turning our collective wisdom into action in meaningful ways.

The third section of this book will bring the understandings gained in the second part into the real world and introduce you to the Three Cs Loop: *create* (yet keep renewing), *connect* (yet keep disconnecting), and *capitalize* (yet keep acting). Together, these Three Cs are the knowledge-based competencies that comprise the "how" of Knowledge Mindfulness: it's by continuously cycling through them that we elevate our knowledge maturity and make Knowledge Mindfulness a practical and powerful force in our organizations, our leadership, and our daily lives.

I started out by saying that the chaos of a world in transition had felt, to me, like an unexpected gift. That doesn't mean it always felt easy or straightforward! But out of the difficulties I faced, I gained a fresh perspective on the uses and power of elevated knowledge—and a new understanding that, I believe, has the power to help us all to lead more effectively and live more fulfilling and joyful lives along the way.

I know that over the past few years, my own journey has led me in startling new directions and left me more focused and energized than ever before. I hope that in the pages that follow, you'll find ways to apply Knowledge Mindfulness in ways that help you, too, to chart a clearer path through our fast-changing world—and to unlock powerful new ways of operating in your professional and personal life.

Chapter 1

The Need for Knowledge Mindfulness

August 2, 1990, is a day that's vividly engraved in my memory. My husband and I had arrived in Kuwait City from Boston just two days before: we were young and just embarking on busy new lives, and we didn't pay much attention to Saddam Hussein blustering away in neighboring Iraq. Nobody did. As my father put it, the Iraqi dictator's saber rattling was nothing more than a "summer cloud" in an otherwise azure sky.

But that morning in August, we awoke to the news that our country had been invaded. Iraqi troops had taken over our city. My husband grabbed some cash and ran to the grocery store—normally a five-minute walk from our home. He was gone for three hours. While I waited for him to return, I stepped outside to see an Iraqi helicopter roaring in just over my head. Through the open side doors, I could see commandos inside with rifles in their hands. I was terrified: my world was crumbling before my eyes, and I had no idea how to make sense of it all.

For all Kuwaitis the invasion was an incredibly difficult experience. But it was also a powerful catalyst. It prompted many people to move forward in a new way, with a different mindset. Some thrived, doing better than they had before the invasion. Others struggled and never truly regained their footing.

Why did some people succeed where others failed? It's a question that continued to haunt me in the years that followed. We all had the same basic resources and opportunities. When catastrophe struck, why did some Kuwaitis prove resilient while others floundered?

Since the COVID-19 pandemic, I've been asking that question again. The whole world has faced massive disruption. Once again some organizations, institutions, and businesses have crumbled and shut down. Others have struggled but survived; a few have managed to find opportunities for growth and advancement.

These aren't just abstract questions. They are urgent inquiries that we need to confront in order to cope with an increasingly uncertain and unstable world. The invasion of Kuwait and the COVID-19 pandemic are just two examples of the disruption we now face. We live in unprecedented times, and for all of us—as individuals, as organizations, and as leaders—the challenges are only just beginning.

Welcome to the VUCA World

Thousands of years ago, in a small town on the coast of modern-day Turkey, a Greek philosopher named Heraclitus needed just two words to expound a remarkable doctrine: πάντα ρέι, or *panta rhei.*

These words can be translated simply as "everything flows" or "life is flux." Change, Heraclitus tells us, is the only constant: no matter how hard you try, you can't step in the same river twice.

If that lesson was relevant 2,500 years ago—when books were laboriously transcribed by hand, buildings took decades to build, and triremes were the cargo ships of the day—it's all the more important for today's leaders. The river of which Heraclitus spoke has become a raging torrent of disruption, sweeping away everything in its path. Change is happening faster than ever before. Even the rate of change is accelerating: it took thousands of years for humanity to invent the printing press, but only four hundred years more to invent the telephone—and then just thirty-three more to create the first computer.

We're now seeing *exponential* change and the integration of *new* technologies. That's where the unpredictability comes in! We aren't progressing steadily, in a linear way: everything intersects and overlaps. Moore's law has moved beyond microchips: each new innovation drives *other* innovations and triggers breakthroughs in *other* fields of study, accelerating change across the entire ecosystem.

This presents enormous challenges for today's leaders. There are no models to prepare us for what lies ahead and no way to predict the speed and extent of the change we'll face in the coming decades. Only one thing is certain: change will be enormous, staggering, incomprehensible. The old approaches will no longer work, and we have no new models to prepare us for what lies ahead.

Military leaders describe this kind of fast-changing environment as **volatile, uncertain, complex, and ambiguous (VUCA)**. That's become a buzzword in man-

> *There are no models to prepare us for what lies ahead and no way to predict the speed and extent of the change we'll face in the coming decades.*

agement training circles, and I'll continue to use the term in this book—there's no need to reinvent the wheel.

By definition the VUCA world is unpredictable, multidimensional, and difficult to comprehend. Huge threats and opportunities arise out of nowhere: you never know when the phone will ring with life-changing news. Just as volatile chemicals sometimes blow up in your face, so the VUCA world is prone to spasms and seismic shifts that change the operating environment in unpredictable and extreme ways. We need to find a path to optimism and hope—but that can feel very hard amid so much chaos!

Adding to the challenge, the VUCA world is more than just complicated: it's also profoundly complex. Complicated is a car engine: lots of moving parts but ultimately mechanistic and predictable. Complex is the city that the car drives through: sprawling, organic, interconnected, and deeply chaotic. The problems of the past were merely complicated, but today every new discovery or challenge has more facets to understand than most of us can wrap our minds around.

As business leaders we see this in countless areas. Financial markets, for instance, are incredibly complex, dependent not just on the behavior of corporations and customers, but also on geopolitical and macroeconomic trends, the emotional state of investors, new technologies ranging from crypto to high-speed trading, rumors, and even the weather. We increasingly rely on automation to manage markets, introducing further complexity as investors and regulators seek to make sense of a world in which algorithms can execute tens of thousands of trades in a single second.

Supply chains are another example of complexity in action. At this very moment, millions of shipping containers are crisscrossing the world's oceans; every year, the US imports over 50 million containers carrying everything from iPhones to frozen food.[4] But even that sprawling network of shipments is only part of the story: from the impact of COVID-19 on factories in China or Indonesia, to unpredictable surges or slumps in consumer demand, to extraordinary events such as freighters getting jammed sideways in the Suez Canal, getting products from A to B on schedule is an incredibly complex business.

Dealing with this kind of complexity isn't easy for us as individuals—and it's even harder for us as business leaders, given the increased responsibilities today's leaders have to shoulder. In today's world the corner office isn't just a place where meetings are held. It's the place where leaders have to keep track of a changing world, stay abreast of digital transformation, think about issues of diversity and inclusion, and make smart decisions.

Leadership responsibilities are changing exponentially, and it can be hard for bosses to keep up. Between 2000 and 2019, according to McKinsey's *CEO Excellence*, the average tenure of CEOs in the United States has fallen from ten years to less than seven; over the same period, global executive turnover rates have increased from roughly 13 percent to almost 18 percent.[5] More than ever, today's leaders report feeling lonely, overwhelmed, and burned out. Organizations are failing to attract new talent and retain employees, and the Great Resignation, depression, anxiety, stress, and other mental health problems are just a few of the challenges increasingly facing leaders in a VUCA world. To turn that around, leaders need light, they need clarity, and they need a way forward through the coming storms.

The Road Forward

To chart a way forward as both leaders and individuals, we need to work first on understanding the world we are living in. Only then can we start to imagine the future we face.

This is an active process: whether changes are externally or internally triggered, we have the power to decide how we'll interpret and respond to them. Consider, for instance, the story of Jean-Dominique Bauby, a French journalist and editor who suffered a massive stroke and was left almost completely paralyzed. Blinking one eye became his only means of communicating with the outside world. Bauby had no say over the catastrophe that befell him. But instead of giving up, he chose to adapt and to evolve his life in a new direction.

Bauby spent hours each day composing a book in his head, then painstakingly blinking his thoughts to an assistant who counted off letters—A, B, C—to translate his blinks into words. His memoir, *The Diving Bell and the Butterfly*, became a bestseller and a successful movie—in part because it dramatically illustrates our ability to adapt and evolve in the face of even the most drastic of changes if we have the right *understanding* and the strength of will to find a positive way forward.

For leaders, finding that understanding and strength of will often means embracing change in order to unlock new possibilities. What if embracing change meant *interpreting* change as a natural expansion of life—an evolution to something better suited to the new conditions we find ourselves in?

I've seen that in my own life: in my thirties, after ten years as a full-time mother, I began to feel I needed to do more—to evolve and expand my horizons. I pursued a master's degree despite knowing I'd be at a disadvantage because of my unconventional journey. I gathered my courage and invited change into my life.

Bigger changes and new evolutions followed: when I graduated in the top percentile of my class, my professors approached me and said, "Laila, we're a small department. Go get your PhD in the United States, then come back and work with us." After discussing it with my family, I took the leap. My husband kept working in Kuwait while I took our young children to Pittsburgh for three years. It was the biggest self-chosen change of my life, one that truly stretched my evolution and expansion to new levels.

I was forty by the time I returned to Kuwait, PhD in hand, to begin work as a professor. Now, in my fifties, I'm rewiring my life again, leaving academia to write this book and launch a business— another stage in my evolution and expansion! At an age when my mother was thinking about retirement, I'm excited to be following a new path—a recalibration in response to the sweeping changes that have seemed to shake the whole universe since the COVID-19 pandemic began.

Such experiences are increasingly common. Breakthroughs in medical science mean that each generation will live longer than the last; perhaps it made sense for Grandpa to hold one job and retire at sixty-five, but in today's fast-changing world, most of us will have much longer-lasting and more varied careers. The historian Yuval Noah Harari points out that people once built identities that were like stone fortresses, with deep foundations. "Now it makes more sense to build identities like tents that you can fold and move elsewhere," Harari says. "Because we don't know where you will have to move, but you *will* have to move."[6]

The flip side of all this flexibility is that the identities we're building today—and the knowledge that underlies those identities—won't be the same ones we need five years, or maybe even five months, from now. In a VUCA world, systems of knowledge are constantly being tested to breaking point—or breakthrough point—and expanding in new directions to overcome new challenges.

That means the "half-life" of existing knowledge is shrinking: what's known today will be stale tomorrow. By some estimates, an engineering degree is now "fresh" for only four years, meaning every engineer has to upskill on a regular basis. For medical students the sell-by date is even shorter: best practices learned just eighteen to twenty-four months ago may already be out of date.

Already, organizations are hiring not for on-the-job experience—which is outdated almost as soon as it's acquired—but for metaskills that enable people to adapt and evolve. A college education is less valuable than it once was, because its teachings are likely to be stale by the time a student graduates. According to a recent Deloitte study, 90 percent of executives now prioritize flexible skills rather than education or experience—and as a result their organizations are more likely to innovate, retain high performers, and respond effectively to change.[7]

The road forward for today's leaders is to unlock and grow those skills and attributes effectively and to aggregate them in meaningful ways. That means understanding how to create a nurturing environment for a multigenerational workforce, simultaneously leveraging the energy and fresh perspectives of youth and the insights and expertise of older workers. It means finding new ways to engage and inspire employees who see their job not as a destination, but as a stepping stone on a longer journey. Crucially, it also means interpreting change as a natural process of evolution and expansion and knowing how to respond positively and proactively rather than reactively seeing any change as negative.

To carry that positive attitude forward, through the Sturm und Drang of the VUCA world, we need to learn to break free from old habits. Habits, after all, are a kind of defensive mechanism: faced with ambiguity and uncertainty, we instinctively fall back on what we already know and retreat back into our comfort zone. It's been estimated that of the sixty thousand or so different thoughts that cross our minds each day, less than 10 percent are original; the rest are repetitions of thoughts we've previously had.[8] These repeated thoughts grind pathways into our brains, like footprints worn into old stone steps, making it easier for our thoughts to follow those paths again in the future.

That can be valuable: our brain's ability to interpret the world, manage our bodies, use language, or play a musical instrument springs from its ability to distill experiences into habits. But in a VUCA world, we can't afford to get stuck in the same old groove. We need to be able to access or develop smarter, more responsive, and more creative solutions to the new challenges we face now and those we'll face in the future.

We may also need to be able to access or create those smart, responsive solutions *fast,* without having time for the luxury of sitting down and trying to think our way through every new challenge in a slow, rational, and deliberative way. If you accidentally touch a hot plate, your reflexes kick in, and you jerk your hand away almost before you know what's happening. But amid the fast-paced, complex world of today and tomorrow, we can't always rely on our primordial "lizard brain" to generate timely, smart, sophisticated solutions in the moments when we most need them.

What's needed, for both individuals and organizations, is a new understanding of change and of how to *respond* to change instead of simply reacting to it. We need a way to break out of old habits and unlock new solutions—and to do so in a way that's just as fast and fluid as our hardwired responses.

The good news is that we can achieve all these goals, and hit many birds with one stone, by focusing on knowledge. But there's a catch: we can't achieve this simply by relying on our old understanding of knowledge. Instead, we need a new, more comprehensive and expanded understanding—one that bridges the gaps between our multidimensional self and the outside world, to rapidly deliver sophisticated and creative responses to new situations and new challenges.

A New Perspective on Knowledge

People might be the building blocks of organizational knowledge, but that isn't *all* that they are. People are also *people*—people who love, laugh, cry, have wonderful or lousy days, have passions and hobbies, and have vastly different experiences and ways of looking at the world. The academic discipline of knowledge management—even with personal knowledge management added to the mix—felt like it was only scratching the surface. Like a bright spotlight, it illuminated a tiny circle; surely, I felt, if we could light up the rest of the landscape, we could find new ways of thinking about knowledge, ourselves, our organizations, and our lives.

Part of the problem, I realized, was that we had grown too focused on sensory knowledge—the things we perceive, and reason about, using the rational side of our cognitive abilities. This led us to think of knowledge as being the contents and capabilities of our brains—but it's so much more than that! The totality of our knowledge doesn't just reside in our heads. It exists in our hearts and our souls, too, reflecting not just the intellect in isolation, but also the integration of our intuition, other dimensions that we'll explore in the next part, and the complex processes that determine what we attend to and draw inward from the outside world.

So what do we mean by the "totality of our knowledge"? We mean not just the sum of our internal and external knowledge, but also everything that shapes (and, crucially, *emerges from*) the relationships and connections that intermediate the internal and the external. We mean, too, the full richness of our internal selves, expressed not simply as a singular and monolithic "self" but as something much richer and more plural—something itself made up of interconnections and networks of internal relationships.

Our internal knowledge, according to the new perspective I'm proposing, is the knowledge that emerges from all the multidimensional layers of our self, from our head, heart, and soul: it's our intellect, physiology, psychology, and core values. External knowledge, for the sake of simplicity, can be considered the stuff that *other* people know and can share—books, podcasts, movies, speech, conversations, and the broader social or political or economic context within which we operate. It's by grasping these two holistically in all their richness and interconnectedness, rather than viewing them through a reductive lens, that we can expand our perspective on knowledge and thus arrive at a new perspective on knowledge management too.

From Knowledge Management to Knowledge Mindfulness

One of the key insights that Knowledge Mindfulness offers is the integration of an additional domain—self—to the outdated conception of individual knowledge outlined above and its interconnection with the external world. It also, crucially, adds a new emphasis on the importance of reasoning and intuition as equally important aspects of the **totality of our knowledge.**

So the totality of our internal and external knowledge comprises "all that we know," from what we are mindful of in the external world to our self-knowledge that makes up "all that we are"—our body, our personality (including our emotions, ego, and sense of self), and our spirit (or core human values). It's by expanding our knowledge *into* these domains and bringing these critical areas—what we know, not only from the external world but also through our self—into a rich and ongoing dialogue that we can unlock our full potential.

> *One of the key insights Knowledge Mindfulness offers is the integration of an additional domain—self—to the outdated conception of individual knowledge and its interconnection with the external world.*

This represents, in some ways, an evolution beyond traditional conceptions of knowledge management, toward one more suited to the complexities and uncertainties of the world we're living in—one that can bring coherence and impact not only to the external world around us, but also to our inner sense of self-harmony and fulfillment.

28

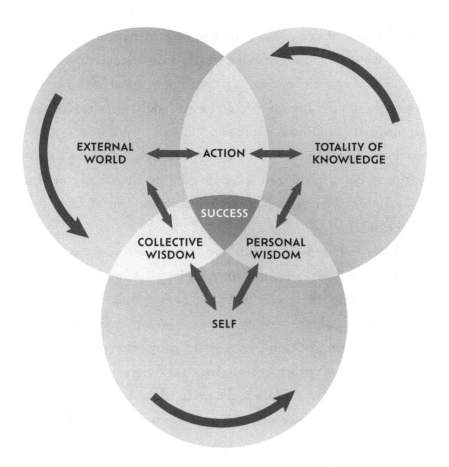

This process doesn't mean disconnecting from the internal-external dynamic that governs our knowledge. It means brokering new, richer, and more powerfully complex connections between all the different knowledge resources available to us, including those we have hitherto been neglecting. It also means augmenting our human intelligence.

To see how that works, notice that by introducing a third circle we've also necessarily revealed new dynamic spaces in which interaction and exchange are possible between the three domains. Where self and knowledge intersect, we find a *window* to **personal wisdom**: the ability to leverage our values, belief, and all our multidimensional self to make sense of and pay attention to what matters in the external world, while also using our hard-earned experiences to reshape, expand, and evolve ourselves on a deep and personal level. Let's not forget that it's the space where exchanges and transformations *can* happen, but it still takes careful and mindful work to realize that possibility. In a VUCA world, knowing those exchanges *can* happen isn't good enough: we can't leave anything to chance! We need to make those exchanges happen and to make them happen faster than ever before.

Where self and the external world intersect, we see **collective wisdom**—or, again, a *window* to collective wisdom—reflecting the potential to bring perspective and insight to our connection with the external world, whether that connection is with people or otherwise. It also reflects the ability to leverage third-party perspectives about us and our behavior and attributes to enrich and elevate our self-understanding. Collective wisdom is the space where we come to realize that our personal values aren't universal truths and that other ways of thinking and knowing can *also* have real value and exert impactful change on the world around us.

Finally, where self, totality of knowledge, and external world intersect, we have the chance to achieve what I term "**success**." It's at this sweet spot, where personal and collective wisdom and action converge, that we can leverage *all* our knowledge with integrity, compassion, focus, and purpose for the benefit of *all*. It's something rather like what sports psychologists call "the zone"—the space in which using knowledge effectively becomes effortlessly clear and joyful and impactful, instead of anxious, fraught, and chaotic. In this space leaders can find success—tangible and intangible, short term and long term—and also drive success for others around them, from their employees to their organization and their immediate ecosystem and the broader world.

We'll explore each of these aspects in more detail later. For now, though, it's important to understand that the chaos of the VUCA world reflects the spinning apart of the totality of our knowledge and the world around us. As these two things grow decoupled—because the world is more complex than the knowledge we're using to understand it!—they fall out of phase: we start to feel lost, adrift, alienated. We can't make sense of the world, and that creates anxiety, fear, and the feeling that we're losing control. Our limited knowledge resources aren't sufficient to help us find our way!

That's the problem that Knowledge Mindfulness is trying to solve. By bringing multifaceted individual and integrative human values and identity back into our discussion of knowledge, it's possible to weave the internal and the external back together and anchor them in a common reference point. It's possible to bring the whole together and to bring coherence and growth not only for the individual leader, but also for everyone who's impacted by their presence and their actions.

For people living in a VUCA world, this is a bit like finding solid ground in the middle of a lake of quicksand. The world around you is constantly changing, so you need to change and evolve too. Not everybody understands that need, though, and even those who do often don't know how or where to begin. That feeling of being out of step with the changing world leads to feelings of stress and confusion. If you understand the connections between yourself, your knowledge, and the external world, though, you can use that clarity as a compass to guide you and help you confidently and proactively embrace change both in yourself and the world around you.

Archimedes claimed he could move the world if he only had a long enough lever and a firm place to stand. Well, Knowledge Mindfulness gives you just that—a firm place to stand, even amid the chaos of a VUCA world, and also a space in which you (and other knowledge-mindful people) can grow and evolve. It's through embracing that evolution, in fact, that you can use all your knowledge and understanding (and those of trusted people around you) to achieve the results you desire.

Why Leaders Need Knowledge Mindfulness

I'm suggesting that Knowledge Mindfulness can be seen as a framework and a practice that focuses on the dynamic relationships between knowledge, self, and the external world to drive more enriching success. It enables us to consciously and continuously expand and evolve our knowledge and thereby make smarter decisions to drive both tangible change in the world and intangible fulfillment in ourselves. When you live and lead with Knowledge Mindfulness, you can operate more purposefully and achieve more meaningful and sustainable success—both for yourself and for those around you.

Knowledge Mindfulness means having the courage to shift our attention and our understanding away from fragmented or narrow understandings that no longer serve us and to refocus on more holistic ways of knowing to unlock more fulfilling paths forward. Knowledge Mindfulness is also a way of awakening ourselves to the river of knowledge that flows through our lives and in which we're swimming—a way of recognizing and reconfiguring the riverbanks (the structures, organizations, rules, blind spots, habits, and assumptions) that simultaneously define and limit the places that our knowledge can carry us.

How, then, does it help business leaders, and the organizations they run, to chart a better path through a VUCA world?

In part Knowledge Mindfulness mirrors the broader shift toward more purposeful and value-driven leadership and organizations. Milton Friedman might have argued that companies existed solely to drive profits for their shareholders, but in today's world both consumers and investors are increasingly looking for companies that align with their values. Sustainability, ethical sourcing and labor practices, employee health and well-being—these aren't merely nice-to-haves in today's business world. Increasingly, they are the key drivers of enduring success. It's hard to bring values into the flow of leadership unless you understand, internalize, and prioritize those values, on both the personal and organizational levels.

Knowledge Mindfulness makes it easier to lead with purpose and integrity and also to forge real human connections with those within and beyond your organization. Instead of simply viewing knowledge as one more component in a mechanistic organization that simply requires maintenance and direction, Knowledge Mindfulness helps leaders to identify the things that matter most to them, draw on other people's perspectives to refine and guide their own viewpoints, and find the clarity of purpose needed to chart a more meaning-ful and deliberate path forward. Knowledge Mindfulness is not only concerned with sustainability, but also with evolution: not only with our self-growth, but also the growth of our employees and organiza-tions. That's what makes this framework so useful in so many ways.

This might sound a bit esoteric, but the reality is that Knowledge Mindfulness is deeply practical: among other things it provides a better approach to drive meaningful bottom-line results for today's businesses.

In a VUCA world, for businesses as well as individuals, adaptability and innovation are the keys to survival and growth. But change is hard, and executing change effectively is rarely a purely intellectual problem. It's also an *emotional* and *spiritual* problem. A lack of so-called "soft" leadership skills relating to people, values, and culture is the key roadblock to effective change management, both internally and externally. The best CEOs and leaders make a point of not only taking personal responsibility for those aspects of their business, but also actually applying these skills in the work they do as leaders. Instead of outsourcing the "fluffy stuff" to HR, they lean in, treat the soft stuff as their top priority, and actually integrate it into their lives.

As Peter Drucker once said, culture eats strategy for breakfast. But you can't build culture simply by optimizing information flows through your business. You need a real, human approach to knowledge—one that's anchored in a strong sense of who you are; of where you're going; of how you're connected to others, your organization, and your society; and of how you want to bring others with you on that journey.

Knowledge Mindfulness, in other words, isn't about simply achieving some kind of satori and then sitting smugly on a mountaintop. The goal—*success*—is the place where personal wisdom, collective wisdom, and action all intersect, enabling you and other trusted people around you to act more purposefully and compassionately to realize powerful and meaningful change in the world and within yourself.

With Knowledge Mindfulness you're better equipped to find the small inflection points that let you spark big changes—and the human connections and empathy that ensure those changes bring benefits to everyone. I was struck recently by a news report about a student in India who'd seen two young bullocks struggling to haul a heavy cart. That's something one sees every day in many parts of India, and most people never give it a second thought. But the student, animated by compassion, was able to really *see* the situation in front of him—and realized that it was possible to ease the bullocks' burden by adding a single wheel to support the yoke.

The result: a kinder way to haul goods, but also a more efficient method that lets farmers get more value from their beasts of burden. The value of compassion, in this case, drove innovation and created a win-win for everyone—a reminder that even in a VUCA world, it's possible to make a real difference when you build bridges between your core values, your intuitions, your rational mind, and the world around you.

A Better-Suited Approach

This book is intended to be both a wake-up call and a practical guide for CEOs and other senior business leaders who need all the human intelligence they can get and who want to change the way they think about and use knowledge and who want to help their employees and their organizations to use knowledge in more effective ways. I hope it will also inspire young professionals and future leaders to chart a path toward more meaningful ways of identifying and achieving their personal and professional goals—so that when they look back on their careers, they'll know they've given their all to a mission they truly believe in.

Why should business leaders pay attention to Knowledge Mindfulness? Well, just look at what happens when a CEO *doesn't* operate with Knowledge Mindfulness. Consider, for instance, Microsoft CEO Satya Nadella's decision in 2014 to tell a room full of college students that women should "have faith" that they'll be compensated fairly and shouldn't ask for raises. "That's good karma," he reassured them, adding that declining to speak up and demand gender equity was actually a "superpower" for professional women.[9]

Unsurprisingly, Nadella's comments drew a major backlash, forcing him to launch a PR blitz and send out a companywide mea culpa in a bid to restore his personal brand. But why did Nadella make such a clumsy comment in the first place? It was, in large part, I think, because he didn't stop to question and step outside of what he thought he knew. He needed to scrutinize his values, especially relating to women, in order to see them for what they were and start to change them. That's what can happen if you lack the wisdom to interrogate the context and foundations of your own understanding—or to look beyond your own beliefs and explore other ways of thinking.

A more knowledge-mindful CEO might have questioned their own beliefs from the get-go and asked whether they were slipping into comforting but incorrect assumptions about how the world works. Or they might have taken a moment to think more clearly and respectfully about their audience's beliefs and ask how their own knowledge should be informed by those of other people with different life experiences. Or they might have gone ahead and made a controversial statement regardless—but have done so deliberately and carefully, in the service of some larger goal.

Instead, Nadella stuck to what he thought he knew and wound up paying the price for it. In the days and weeks that followed, he had to work to reevaluate the things he thought he knew, reengage with the people he'd made to feel unheard, and—with the help of his crisis PR team—turn those learnings into a new kind of leadership anchored in a more mindful understanding of his own core values.

"The fundamental realization that was pretty deep for me was how out of touch I was to … answer the question based on my experience, versus having a deeper empathy for the context of the question," Nadella later reflected. "That's why the answer I gave was a complete nonsense answer. The question was not about what worked for me, or how I approached things. It was about what should someone do when you have a system that actually doesn't work for them."[10]

It was out of that introspection and commitment to learning from others—out of personal wisdom that opened the door to collective wisdom—that Nadella was able to move on from the PR catastrophe he'd brought down upon himself. He committed to creating a culture of growth and learning and turning Microsoft into a place where people asked questions instead of assuming they already knew the answers. "The fact that I could stumble and make that mistake, it got me to think, 'Wow, this is really something you've got to think about much more deeply.' My responsibility has become much more clear to me," Nadella said.

Through his missteps, Nadella was forced to turn inward and then turn outward. That's the critical dynamic at the heart of Knowledge Mindfulness: honest self-appraisal and a commitment to reaching out and understanding yourself through the eyes of others and to learning to understand your knowledge through new viewpoints and perspectives.

In an era of Big Data and artificial intelligence, with machines able to turn vast data sets into actionable insights in the blink of an eye, what place is there for people? The answer surely lies in refocusing on the things that only people can do. Machines can make sense of data, but only people can approach knowledge with humanity, compassion, vision, creativity, and empathy. Artificial intelligence, by its nature, is digital: it sees the world in terms of *yes* or *no*. People view the world in more complex and holistic ways—not just "yes" and "no," but also "maybe"—and that lets them see possibilities (and threats!) that machines are blind to.

> *The critical dynamic at the heart of Knowledge Mindfulness is honest self-appraisal and a commitment to reaching out and understanding yourself through the eyes of others and to learning to understand your knowledge through new viewpoints and perspectives.*

The very things that Nadella was missing are the same critical capabilities that *all* leaders need to cultivate in order to succeed in our fast-changing world. Of course, as Nadella perhaps now realizes, Knowledge Mindfulness isn't something to simply achieve and move on from. It's a journey. But by embarking on that journey, you can avoid some of the painful lessons that come from *not* practicing Knowledge Mindfulness—and you can leverage your new understandings, your wisdom, and your contextual empathy to lift yourself, your employees, and your organization to new heights. *That,* more than anything, is why every CEO needs to learn to lead and act with Knowledge Mindfulness.

Why Knowledge Mindfulness Matters

The knowledge-mindful leader doesn't just know how to avoid embarrassing PR snafus. They have a deeper understanding of their abilities and of the knowledge-based competencies needed to survive and thrive in today's fast-changing world and to adapt and grow into the many different roles they're required to play over their career.

A knowledge-mindful leader is both knowledge literate (in that they understand the interconnections between their knowledge, their business, and their life) and knowledge smart (in that they can apply the totality of their knowledge effectively and intelligently). In exploring Knowledge Mindfulness, you'll learn to leverage both traits, enabling you to bring your augmented intelligence to your work and your community, to set more meaningful goals, and to achieve them.

You'll come to understand, for instance, that chaotic times require us to think in nonlinear ways and to find proactive and creative solutions to the changing world around us. That means taking charge of creating our own reality, looking beyond the surface to set goals that align with our own deeper purpose—and maintaining and renewing the knowledge we gather and leverage along the way. Fail in that, and we could quickly become as stale as last week's loaf of bread.

Beyond the ability to adapt to a fast-changing world, and to maintain a strong sense of their own values as they do so, the knowledge-mindful leader is equipped for a world of lifelong knowing and continual realignment into new roles. They are also infused with a sense of their own connectedness to the world around them—a vital capability, given the degree to which loneliness and isolation currently drive many young (and not so young) professionals into depression, anxiety, and other mental health problems.

By bringing Knowledge Mindfulness to others, such leaders help to train and lead happier, more loyal, and more creative workforces and to attract talented people to their organizations. With a holistic view of themselves and their context and a deep connection with their own reality, the knowledge-mindful leader is profoundly present in the world—and that allows them to lead more effectively and to inspire others to reach higher and to act decisively without losing sight of their strategic goals.

The bottom line: Knowledge Mindfulness brings out the best in us as leaders and equips us to bring out the best in others too. That's good for us and good for our organizations. Whether you're currently a leader or simply hope to become one, Knowledge Mindfulness is is the augmented human-centered approach and toolkit you need to succeed.

The Broader Impact of Knowledge Mindfulness

Knowledge Mindfulness shouldn't be seen as a shortcut to the top of your profession or to achieving excellence as a leader. It can help with those things, but Knowledge Mindfulness isn't just about getting to the pinnacle faster. Rather, it's about making sure that you're climbing the *right* mountain and that you aren't climbing alone. It's by coming together that we'll survive and thrive—reaching the heights to which we aspire and still knowing who we are and what matters to us when we reach the top.

Consider Elvis: the undisputed King, he achieved fame, wealth, adulation, and critical acclaim on a scale that none of us can hope to rival. But he died alone, depressed, and unhappy—because in climbing so high, he lost track of what really mattered and alienated himself from those around him. Paranoid and angry, he built barriers instead of bridges—only to find that the adoring crowds, in the end, were no substitute for real human connections. "I'm just so tired of being Elvis Presley," the King told anyone who'd listen. "Those people don't love me in a personal way. They don't know what's inside me."[11]

By way of contrast, consider Steve Jobs. The Apple founder wasn't seen as a people person; in fact he was known for his brusqueness and egotism, and he annoyed and alienated plenty of people on his way to the top. But as he grew as a person and as a leader, he became less bristly, less isolated, and started growing both more focused about his goals and more generous and outward looking in how he lived and led. That was especially true as his health failed: in the last months of his life, Jobs showed remarkable empathy and was eager to spend his finite time and energy helping others with the problems they faced.

What set Elvis and Steve Jobs on such different trajectories? For Jobs it was the realization—much like my own, when I fled Kuwait all those years ago—that in an uncertain world, the things that matter most aren't actually *things* at all. As Jobs liked to say, the goal isn't to be the richest man in the cemetery: "In the broadest sense, the goal is to seek enlightenment—however you define it."[12]

The challenge, though, is that you can't achieve that enlightenment—you can't even really *define* enlightenment in a meaningful way—if you're stuck in the VUCA world with the traditional understanding of knowledge and knowledge management.

To reach higher—in your work, in your personal life, and in any other areas that matter to you—you need to consciously evolve and expand your knowledge and understanding, in an integrative way, to better grasp yourself, the world around you, and the interconnections between the two. You need to strive for an understanding of who you are, what matters to you, and what your deepest needs and desires and beliefs add up to. You also need to reach out to others and find a path forward that lets you give and teach as much as you learn and take, so you can not only have an impact in the world, but also manifest your own self and identity in profound and meaningful ways.

When I'm talking about "success," then, I'm not just talking about reaching the top of the mountain. For me, "success" is less about arriving somewhere than about what you see when you get there and how you use that to drive value for both yourself and others. That might mean tangible success in a specific endeavor; it might also mean intangible forms of value, such as finding a way to stand in joy, composure, and calmness amid the chaos of the current moment. Knowledge Mindfulness, ultimately, inspires us to step into new leadership roles focused on coaching others, listening to their needs, and unlocking real benefits. The upshot: you'll enable people to evolve and grow both in their work and as human beings, and all the while you'll be evolving and growing too.

Crucially, you'll also learn how to unlock Knowledge Mindfulness in others, based on the understanding that either we all swim together, or we drown alone. You'll learn to unite your organization to drive success, while still appreciating and nurturing the uniqueness of its component parts. After all, no matter how high your knowledge lets you climb, it will mean nothing if you're alone when you get to your destination. Knowledge Mindfulness is fundamentally about connecting more deeply with ourselves and others—and it's by forging those deeper connections with head and heart and soul and transmuting collective knowledge into meaningful action that you'll unlock your organization's full potential.

In the chapters that follow, we'll dig into all these areas in more detail. In part two we'll zoom in to look more closely at different components of knowledge, our selves, and the external world—then in part three we'll zoom back out to look at how they work together as an engine. Remember, it can be rewarding to zoom in on different elements and work to understand them better—but it's through the *interconnection* of these elements, and their integration into a cohesive whole, that the magic really happens.

Part 2:

Zooming In:
The Elements of
Knowledge Mindfulness

Chapter 2

Understanding Knowledge

How many times have you heard someone say, "I know!" or "I don't know!" without giving it a second thought? We *use* knowledge all the time, which makes it all the more perplexing that knowledge itself—what it is, what it does, how it really works—can be remarkably hard to get a proper handle on.

Plato, one of the first philosophers to really dig into the idea of knowledge, recognized the slipperiness of the topic and how easy it is to think you understand knowledge when in fact you've barely scratched the surface. Imagine you live in a cave, with all your perceptions and ideas merely shadows flickering on the wall. True reality, Plato wrote, is what lies *outside* the cave, casting the shadows that we mistake for truth.

Countless other thinkers have tried to pursue, pin down, and understand knowledge. They've bequeathed us endless different definitions and interpretations of knowledge, each reflecting different ways that people have seen or understood knowledge—from the

Platonic idea of knowledge as a justified true belief to simply understanding gained from experience. In fact academics have created an entire discipline—"epistemology"—to try to explain what knowledge is and how it works.

Even the linguistics of knowledge vary widely. In French, to know can be *connaître* or *savoir*, depending on whether what you know is personal ("Do you know Jim?") or book learning ("Do you know how to conjugate this verb?"). The ancient Greek word *gnosis* is sometimes used for knowledge in the former sense but can also mean spiritual insights and is the root of modern English terms such as "cognition." In Sanskrit, meanwhile, the word for knowledge, *veda*, derives from an early Indo-European word meaning "to see"—the same root that gives us the words "vision" and "wisdom"—and implies a kind of true sight or deep comprehension.

Fortunately, business leaders don't need a PhD in philosophy or linguistics to engage with knowledge in profoundly meaningful ways. In fact part of what leads us astray, when we think about knowledge, is the urge to pin knowledge down—to make it mean one thing and not another. If I believe knowledge *only* means learned information and shut my eyes to *other* kinds of knowledge, I'll lose an awful lot along the way. What we should ask, then, isn't so much "What is knowledge?" but rather "What if knowledge is *more* than I believe it to be?" or "What *kinds* of knowledge work best for the problem I'm facing or the decision I need to make?"

> If I believe knowledge only means learned information and shut my eyes to other kinds of knowledge, I'll lose an awful lot along the way.

This kind of open-minded inquiry is vitally important for today's organizations and today's leaders. The Armenian mystic George Gurdjieff tells us, "Take the understanding of the East and the knowledge of the West—and then seek."[13] The division between East and West might seem a bit contrived to modern ears. (I'm from the Middle East— where does that leave me?!) But Gurdjieff's point—that there's value to be found in both "Western" rationalism and "Eastern" spiritualism and that both are really just starting points for a broader process of inquiry—remains valuable.

Part of what Gurdjieff is getting at, I think, is rediscovering the joy that's to be found in curiosity and inquiry. As a parent I've always loved birthdays. There's little purer than the joy a kid takes in ripping open a carefully wrapped gift. But that excitement is actually a hardwired response—the result of dopamine coursing through our synapses, triggering our reward centers—that exists to drive us forward and entice us to seek growth and new experiences.

That thrill has gone missing from the way most of us think about knowledge today. People confuse information—which is really just organized data—with knowledge, which encompasses a more complex context and meaning than information. As such, they see knowledge as the outcome of education: little more than memorizing rows of dates or the elements of the periodic table. "Knowledge," seen in this light, seems a bit dull and dutiful—it might sometimes be useful, but it isn't *fun* or *exciting*.

One of my core goals in this chapter is to help you rethink what knowledge means and to rekindle that missing spark of excitement. What matters, I'll argue, is not just the narrow learning we get from educational institutions, which is serving us less and less in a VUCA world—it's also the broader ways in which we experience knowledge across the entirety of our lived experiences. Seen through this lens, knowledge isn't narrow, insular, or tedious. It's a living system—a network of different nodes and connections that are continuously being reconfigured. Seen through this lens, knowledge is a spontaneous and exhilarating process of engaging with the world, with others, and with yourself and fusing all those things into a holistic and all-encompassing sense of purpose and energy.

Knowledge, we'll see in the following pages, isn't just about consuming packages of information. It's about curiously and critically ripping off the wrapping, looking *inside* those packages, spotting new connections between one package and another, and reveling in the new sparks that fly as we make each fresh connection. It's time to ask, what happened to the child inside us? How did we get so caught up in the plodding *accumulation* of knowledge that we stopped *playing* and *questioning* and *discovering*?

Part of the problem, I think, is that we allowed ourselves to become governed by self-imposed limits on our natural curiosity and development. When I teach I tell my students there's no such thing as a stupid question. Most young children understand that: they'll ask questions and take joy in hearing the answers. As we get older, though, we lose that courage. We stop asking questions and shrink back out of fear of embarrassment.

It's like a bicycle on a muddy track. We start off unencumbered, whizzing along, but as we move through life, we pick up more and more accumulated ideas about what's permitted or about how the world works—like mud clinging to the wheels of the bike. At home, at school, out in society—we learn what's acceptable and what isn't, what's *possible* and what isn't, and that clouds our perceptions of our world. All too often it slows us down: we forget to be curious and joyful, and we wind up hauling ourselves through a rut, rather than embracing new possibilities.

The path to Knowledge Mindfulness can feel a bit like this. As leaders we all think we know what knowledge is. Depending on how much you've read or how much thought you've given to this problem, you might offer up things like "mindset" or "mental model," or "thinking" or "learning," or even "intelligence" as examples of knowledge.

Those aren't *wrong*, but they aren't complete either—just as the shadows perceived by Plato's cave dwellers' shadows were only a pale reflection of reality. In the pages that follow, I'm going to ask you to accept that what you currently understand about knowledge is actually only a subset of what might be out there. I'm going to ask you to expand your definition of knowledge and to think more deeply about what the *totality* of knowledge might be. Knowledge, I'll argue, is a complex system that we need to understand deeply—which is why it makes sense to spend a chapter talking about it now, even though it's an integral part of the broader holistic framework we're exploring.

That's critical for today's organizations, because in a VUCA world, we can't afford to get stuck in a rut. Next year's challenges will look very different from last year's or this year's. Even our understanding about knowledge will change; today's genius will be tomorrow's idiot unless we keep on elevating our knowledge and ascending—deliberately, curiously, and continuously—toward a more complex form of knowledge that can serve us better.

Knowledge as a Living System

There's an old Sufi story about four beggars who find a single shiny coin in the dust and immediately start fighting over how to spend it. The first beggar, a Persian, insists that they spend the money on *angur*. The next, an Arab, says, "No, we must buy some *inab*." The third beggar, who hails from Turkey, says, "*Inab?* Terrible idea—we need some *üzüm*." The fourth man, a Greek, says, "Rot and nonsense: we must buy *stafylia*." Fortunately, a passing polyglot breaks up the fight. "You idiots—stop fighting and listen to what your friends are really saying. *Angur, inab, üzüm, stafylia*—these are all just different words for the same thing: grapes!"

Those beggars had knowledge—they each knew what they wanted, and they knew the names of the things the other beggars wanted too. But they didn't have the level of understanding needed to solve the problem in front of them. Only when the passerby helped out, providing a higher level of understanding grounded in more complex and interconnected knowledge that integrated their fragmented understandings, did a solution become apparent.

In the pages that follow, I'll describe this level of understanding as one's **knowledge maturity**. It's a term that designates the richness both of our knowledge and of our understanding of that knowledge and especially of the degree to which our knowledge encompasses something complex and plural and multifaceted, rather than something simple and monolithic. The nodes and connections between different elements of our knowledge might sound complicated and confusing—but in fact it's by leveraging those connections, and multiplying and reinforcing them through repetition, that we elevate our knowledge maturity and make our knowledge and our understandings stronger, more resilient, and more powerful.

Of course, as we seek new ways to lead and to leverage knowledge effectively across our organizations, we need to seek out not just *more* knowledge, or even *better* knowledge, but rather *the right* knowledge for the specific challenges we face. Every business owner would prefer to own triple-A-rated investments rather than low-quality junk. Well, we need to elevate our knowledge portfolio, too, and ensure we have triple-A knowledge at our disposal—not just by expanding the scope of our knowledge, but by understanding and enhancing the connections between all the different elements too.

We won't reach that point by trying to specify, define, and constrain our knowledge. Instead, we need to embrace and accept the **totality of knowledge** available to us. That means seeing the complex richness of our knowledge and understanding it as a dynamic living system rather than a static accumulation of facts and information.

According to the Chilean biologists Humberto Maturana and Francisco Varela, all living organisms are fundamentally involved in processes of cognition. "Living systems are cognitive systems, and living as a process is a process of cognition," they argue.[14] This startling insight, known as the Santiago theory of cognition, tells us that knowledge and knowing are themselves ubiquitous and part of every aspect of every living thing: knowledge is the water in which we all swim, and it is as omnipresent as life itself.

Once you see the degree to which knowledge and related cognitive processes saturate our world, you can begin to intuit that systems of knowledge are themselves living and dynamic systems—in constant motion, driven by powerful processes of cross-pollination and reproduction and evolution. Knowledge Mindfulness urges us to recognize and reconcile ourselves with these processes and to understand our knowledge, ourselves, and our contexts as being engaged in a continuous, dynamic, and vibrant interplay.

Embracing this enables us to foreground these processes, rather than having them operate out of sight, and to make all aspects of our systems of knowledge amenable to conscious intervention and change. Our knowledge, when seen as a living system that is, itself, part of a larger living system, can be mindfully pruned, shaped, and utilized to ensure that the entire system of systems of which they're part can flourish and thrive.

What does this mean for how we understand the totality of knowledge? Well, the totality of our knowledge certainly includes data, information, and the things gained from book learning: I spent years studying computer science, among many other areas, and my head is stuffed with facts and theories about everything from the history of computer design to the uses of various programming languages. But if you add up all these things, would you capture the totality of my knowledge? Not even close! There are many things I know that *aren't* encapsulated in this conscious, rational view of knowledge.

In fact the knowledge we consciously acquire and process through our five senses is just the tip of the iceberg. There's a whole lot going on beneath the surface too. I see our knowledge as springing from three key sources: our **conscious mind** (and its rational interpretation of everything that we draw in from our five senses), our **subconscious mind** (and its mediation of rehearsed or reflexive knowledge that comes to us *without* thinking), and our **unconscious mind** (and its surfacing of deep-seated spiritual values that are truly instinctive and part of our DNA).

Together, our subconscious and unconscious knowledge make up what is often referred to as our **intuition**—the quickfire hunches, reflexes, insights, and gut feelings that enable us to operate *without* the laborious process of engaging our conscious mind and rationally thinking things through. In a VUCA world, that's an important asset and one that a knowledge-mindful leader leverages appropriately—not *instead* of slower or more deliberative ways of knowing, but as an important addendum to the broader living system of our knowledge.

Understanding Intuition

The subconscious and unconscious are closely connected, and we may sometimes mistake the one for the other. It's important to remember that the subconscious represents accumulated knowledge that has been rehearsed, practiced, or internalized to such a degree that it becomes second nature; it represents a kind of "deep memory." Learning to engage this deep memory involves not just rational processes, but also emotional ones: how we *feel* is deeply tied up in our processes of recollection, and we need to tame and take charge of that emotional process in order to optimize and leverage our subconscious knowledge.

When you read a sentence in your native language, you can instantly spot a grammatical error. What most people *can't* do, though, is offer up a clear explanation of *why* the sentence is incorrect. As Michael Polanyi puts it, "We know more than we can tell."[15] Much of our most powerful knowledge falls into this category. The longer you spend using and rehearsing knowledge, such as by speaking a language, the more it gets engraved in your memory—and the more it becomes *subconscious* knowledge that can be leveraged fast, with no need for conscious thought. (The downside, of course, is that subconscious knowledge is hard to "unlearn," so we need to be careful—and mindful—about the knowledge we allow to become this ingrained.)

If the subconscious contains knowledge rooted in experience, the unconscious represents knowledge that bubbles up from within: our authentic self, core values, and spiritual DNA. This can feel elusive, but it's the essence of who we are in *relation* to our knowledge: it encapsulates the very blueprint of our being, from our deepest needs and desires to our highest human values. I might rely on my subconscious for my driving skills, but my unconscious is what really keeps me on the straight and narrow.

Now, as humans we love to fragment and label things, but of course the reality is that these different elements actually work *together*, feeding into the *totality* of our knowledge. It's the blend of our conscious mind, our memory and subconscious, and the deep values rising up from our unconscious that determines what we attend to and what kind of information we draw inward from the outside world. Our intuition thus plays a vital role in expanding the totality of our knowledge. It's a bit like that passerby in the Sufi tale: use your intuition well, and all the scattered bits of information and conscious knowledge you've collected become much easier to integrate and understand, and new solutions arise quickly in the moments when you most need them. Your knowledge is much, much more than the information and analyses taking place on the surface. Intuition is the way that your conscious mind drinks from this deeper well—and also the way that entrenched memories and deep human insights bubble up from below to guide you.

This is a continuous process of back and forth. Knowledge, in this sense, can be seen as a kind of cognitive energy that constantly circulates: feeding and fed by the way we relate to the outside world but also feeding and fed by the "inner lens"—intuition!—through which we relate to our subconscious and unconscious knowledge. By building and using knowledge, using our cognitive capabilities, we encourage that process of circulation, driving feedback loops that recall and reinscribe old memories, recenter and reprioritize our core values, and continuously expand and renew the totality of our knowledge.

Expanding the Totality of Your Knowledge

This is a virtuous cycle: the more you use your intuition, the stronger your intuitions become and the more confidence you gain in using your intuition when you need it most. In a VUCA world, there's seldom time to reason and deliberate—so we need to start building these muscles now, so we'll be able to rely on our intuition to drive fast, effective action when it's most needed. Gigerenzer tells us that "the intelligence of the unconscious is in knowing without thinking."[16] This isn't the absence of knowledge—it's the absence of *conscious thought.* When we engage our rational minds, we have to process incoming information, connect it with information retrieved from memory, and analyze it to build knowledge before finally taking action. With intuitive knowledge you can bypass that process and simply *act.*

Other researchers have noted the power of bypassing the rational mind to find solutions quickly. Antonio Damasio calls this "the mysterious mechanism by which we arrive at the solution of a problem without reasoning toward it"—a mechanism, moreover, that is mediated by emotion as much as by any conscious effort. "It is not necessarily the case that the knowledge of the intermediate steps is absent, only that emotion delivers the conclusion so directly and rapidly that not much knowledge need come to mind," Damasio adds. What I describe here as unconscious knowledge Damasio sees as "simply rapid cognition with the required knowledge partially swept under the carpet, all courtesy of emotion and much past practice."[17]

What Damasio misses, though, is the importance of the unconscious as part of the process of intuition: we need both emotional intelligence and spiritual intelligence to effectively leverage "rapid cognition" and make smart, effective, and authentic decisions as we navigate the VUCA world. This might seem to be at odds with conventional Western scientific conceptions of knowledge, but it's really just an application of traditional Western science to the *entirety* of our knowledge. We're raised in a positivist tradition that prizes rationality, and that often leads us to dismiss "fuzzy" concepts such as intuition, emotion, and values, rather than addressing them in a rational way. Ironically, our emotional response to such ideas often prevents us from thinking clearly about them and acting intelligently!

So again, what do we mean when we talk about the totality of our knowledge? We mean everything that springs from our conscious, subconscious, and unconscious minds. Our rational, conscious mind is only half (at most!) of the story: beneath the surface there's more going on. Our intuition isn't in charge, but it's potent, and it shapes our perceptions of and interactions with the world; the conscious mind, meanwhile, is where we develop our intellect and make choices that serve as the framework for subconscious processing. The totality of our knowledge is (obviously) what we know. But it's also the lens through which we see our reality—the outside world and also our own identity and the nature of our relationships with those around us.

To unlock the high-quality knowledge we need, and the rapid knowledge resources that are so vital to success in the VUCA world, we need to expand and evolve all aspects of our knowledge. That means maintaining awareness and upgrading the ways in which we consciously work with information and data to build new knowledge and establish new connections both within ourselves and with the outside world. It means sharpening our recall from memory to more quickly and effectively surface subconscious knowledge. And it means tapping into and strengthening our core values and training our unconscious mind to guide us on that journey.

Get that right, and it's not just about quantity, but quality. We don't just get *more* knowledge—we get knowledge that's more complex and interconnected and thus more flexible and better suited to the kinds of situations we face in a VUCA world.

Unlocking the Totality of Our Knowledge

It's important to understand that the expansion we see as we embrace the totality of our knowledge isn't additive—it's multiplicative, or even exponential. As our knowledge grows more densely interconnected, the elevation of our knowledge or deepening of our understanding in one area ripples out, shedding new light across many other connected aspects of our knowledge and understanding.

This means that accessing the totality of your knowledge, and understanding and learning to add more nodes and strengthen the connections that run through your knowledge, is as transformative as knowing the meaning rather than just the sound of the words you use. It unlocks completely new ways of seeing the world—as a whole, rather than something fragmented—which in turn helps reveal new solutions to previously intractable problems.

It should be easy to see how this lesson applies in the business world. The totality of our knowledge helps us to identify partners with shared interests and rivals that we need to *turn into* partners instead of simply striving to outcompete. It helps us to understand our own needs (and why we need them!) and also those of our counterparts, so that we can strike the best possible deals. And it helps us to recognize, leverage, and strengthen connections to allow knowledge to flow more freely and to elevate and manifest our knowledge maturity through the impact we have on our organization and on the world around us.

But just as knowledge without action is useless, so rational knowledge without insight and intuition is incomplete (and vice versa, of course). We need to unlock and integrate *all* of the totality of our knowledge in order to realize our full potential. Find the key to unlock the power inherent in your knowledge—in the *totality* of your knowledge—and you wind up empowered in ways you couldn't previously have imagined.

In the business world, especially, we've prioritized conscious and rational knowledge building for far too long, while neglecting the intuitive aspects of knowledge building. It's easy to see why: in the business world, things only seem real if you can count them, quantify them, enter them in a spreadsheet, or put them in a PowerPoint deck to show to your investors. Try to explain to your board of directors or to your VC partner that they should take your gut

> *In the business world, things only seem real if you can count them, quantify them, enter them in a spreadsheet, or put them in a Power-Point deck. The reality, though, is that both rational and intuitive knowledge are vital.*

feelings or hunches seriously, and you'll get laughed out of the room. The reality, though, is that both rational and intuitive knowledge are vital and that the two complement each other by equipping us to manage different kinds of situations.

Here are seven points we need to be mindful of if we want to break out of this mindset—and bring the totality of our knowledge, as opposed to the narrower interpretations of knowledge by which most of us have hitherto been guided, to bear on the challenges we face as leaders:

1. Intuition has never been more important.

Complex systems are necessarily hard to make sense of using analytical thinking and reasoning. But chaotic systems are even harder to comprehend: either literally impossible to grasp in their entirety or—even if you *do* know virtually everything about the system—impossible to make predictions about. Chaos theory tells us that a Brazilian butterfly's flapping wings can cause a storm in Texas—but in a VUCA world, it's as though we just moved into a butterfly house. Wings are flapping everywhere; chaos is all around us—and our analytic minds and conscious knowledge simply aren't up to the task.

That means the development of our intuition, and our awareness of and sensitivity to our *inner* knowing, our unconscious and subconscious minds, is urgently required. This isn't just knowing *more*. It's knowing *differently* and looking beyond our raw cognitive functions to find other ways of understanding and solving problems.

In a complex world, it's tempting to look for simple answers and to deal with ambiguities or uncertainties by simply ignoring them. Simplicity is seductive but also reductive: the knowledge-mindful leader knows that knowledge is powerful enough to cope with complexity and to face up to ambiguities and uncertainties without simply dismissing them. Knowledge isn't rigid: it bends instead of breaking and absorbs instead of excluding—and the leader who leans into this and maximizes the totality of their knowledge rather than seeking the brittle comfort of narrower ways of knowing will often find their way to more responsible and impactful solutions.

2. We have a need for speed.

In the ever-changing environment of the VUCA world, you can't sit around contemplating and cogitating—you need to act *now* to avoid disaster. Imagine you're driving on the highway and a deer bounds out into the street ahead of you—you don't have time to consciously think about what's happening. You ride your reflexes, stomp the brakes, and hopefully react in time to avert a collision. In the same way, as leaders in a VUCA world, we need to get used to trusting our intuition and making snap decisions in response to new inputs and sudden changes in the status quo.

For leaders this might sound scary. In fact, though, it should be an exciting proposition—because what we're really talking about is a massively underutilized asset that can confer an enormous and enduring competitive advantage. If you can learn to harness the *totality* of your knowledge, you'll be able to operate with far more speed and confidence than rivals who are only tapping into explicit and conscious knowledge. You'll make better decisions, too, because you're leveraging all the insights available to you—the entire iceberg of knowledge, rather than just the few feet bobbing above the surface.

3. The subconscious gives you shortcuts.

Your subconscious helps you to spot patterns. If you know how to climb one rock face, then you can apply the same techniques and grips to successfully climb another, even if you've never seen it before. In fact you'll probably reach the top while a climbing novice is still standing, baffled, at the base of the cliff.

Roger Schank, a computer scientist at Northwestern University, calls these internalized responses "scripts." Much like the script to a play, or lines of computer code, these scripts are efficient guides to complex situations; by following them we can skip the burdensome process of consciously analyzing every step we make. Scripts, in this way, are nodes in the network that gives rise to intuitive knowledge. But they aren't static; they change over time and are constantly refined as we learn more about ourselves and the world around us. "Scripts are interesting not when they work but when they fail," Schank remarks. "When the waiter doesn't come over with the food, you have to figure out why; when the food is bad or the food is extraordinarily good, you want to figure out why. You learn something when things don't turn out the way you expected."[18]

That's an important insight, because it's a reminder that while intuition can be an important part of (or emerge powerfully from) our spiritual DNA, it isn't magic. We often arrive at intuitive insights by learning the steps so thoroughly that they happen automatically, without conscious thought and therefore at great speed. The psychologist Karl Weick calls intuition "compressed expertise," and that's often true: while intuition *provides* shortcuts, there are no shortcuts to developing intuition.[19] You have to put in the work and earn the insights that you're later able to rely upon.

For leaders this can be a reassuring fact: when you rely on intuition, you aren't just pulling ideas out of the air. You're leveraging all the work you've *already* done and all the knowledge you've gained over the years in which you've been perfecting your skills.

4. The unconscious gives you holistic answers.

Of course, scripts are only useful for situations that you've dealt with before or where a strategy you've previously developed can be applied quickly and neatly to a related problem. In the VUCA world, things are seldom so simple—and that's where your unconscious becomes incredibly important, because it allows you to respond quickly and fluidly in ways that reflect your innermost values, even in situations you haven't seen before.

Picasso once famously charged a million francs for a drawing he sketched on a napkin. "How can you possibly charge so much for something you drew in five minutes?" an onlooker demanded. "You've got it all wrong," Picasso said. "It took me forty years to learn to draw that in five minutes." What Picasso meant wasn't just that it took him forty years to learn to draw. That's part of the story: Picasso certainly had some amazing scripts in place that allowed him to effortlessly paint or draw things without having to think about where to place each line. But Picasso had also spent forty years strengthening his *unconscious* mind: finding his own authentic voice and learning to express himself.

When we look at Picasso's famous "Dove of Peace," we see not just a few expertly scribbled lines. We see Picasso expressing something deep within himself—something that aligns with and reflects his true values and sense of himself. It's that ability to tap into his unconscious on demand that makes Picasso an artist rather than merely a craftsman—and that makes even a spontaneous napkin doodle by Picasso worth paying a million francs for.

As leaders we need to learn to similarly appreciate the value of our knowledge—and to recognize that the insights that come to us in a flash are often, in fact, the result of decades of experience commingled with our core values.

5. Knowledge reflects humbleness.

Weick observes that it's easy for us to grow addicted to the feeling of being right—what he terms the "illusion of accuracy." In a VUCA world, such addictions are especially tempting and especially dangerous. "In a dynamic, competitive, changing environment, illusions of accuracy are short lived, and they fall apart without warning," Weick writes. "Reliance on a single, uncontradicted data source can give people a feeling of omniscience, but because those data are flawed in unrecognized ways, they lead to nonadaptive action."[20]

In other words, donning blinders and sticking to what you know makes you *feel* strong—but it actually makes you weaker. For leaders, truly internalizing this single insight is the key to achieving Knowledge Mindfulness—because it's the spur that will drive you to seek *other* and *better* and *broader* ways of knowing, instead of settling for the cold comforts of what you already believe you know.

Bruce Lee, the martial artist, famously urged people to "be water." Water is formless and shapeless, he explained. "You put water into a cup; it becomes the cup. You put it into a bottle; it becomes the bottle."[21] In much the same way, knowledge is shapeless and formless; it constantly grows and changes and shifts as it interacts with the environment. Like water it's useful, powerful, creative, destructive—

depending on how it's used. And like water it can grow stagnant or simply evaporate away if you don't tend to it and keep it fresh.

We've all met "experts" whose knowledge consists of stock responses and who offer the same answer to any question. If your only tool is a hammer, then every problem looks like a nail. When knowledge stops evolving and questioning and self-examining, it grows stagnant and becomes opinion or dogma instead of real knowledge. In fact, the more knowledgeable one becomes, the more humble one becomes about one's knowledge—because the more clearly one sees its limits. Socrates, remember, famously claimed to know *only* that he knew nothing.

> *The more knowledge-able one becomes, the more humble one becomes about one's knowledge—because the more clearly one sees its limits.*

6. Expand the limits.

Knowledge doesn't happen in a vacuum. It exists within a context, and it includes and incorporates the limitations of what's known. American Secretary of Defense Donald Rumsfeld drew mockery after trying to make this point in relation to the second Gulf War. "As we know, there are known knowns; there are things we know we know. We also know there are known unknowns; that is to say we know there are some things we do not know. But there are also unknown unknowns—the ones we don't know we don't know," he explained.[22]

Rumsfeld's language may have been a bit tortured, but he was referencing an important concept anchored in what psychologists call the Johari window—the attempt to achieve understanding of what you know, what others know, and where the two overlap.

Since what you don't know can hurt you, this awareness is extremely important. If you suffer from allergies, knowing or not knowing what's in a cake could be a matter of life and death. If you make a business trip overseas, not knowing the local significance of a given word or gesture could make the difference between landing a big deal or returning home with nothing to show for your efforts. In the West, for instance, we know that it's important to look the other person in the eye as you speak to them. Try using that "knowledge" in Japan, though, and you'll be seen as disrespectful.

7. Let knowledge flow

Knowledge sometimes seems like a contradiction: it is fluid, intuitive, and hard to capture in words or to comprehend logically—yet it can also be formally structured and consciously acquired. It's this polarity that we need in a VUCA world! At the end of the day, knowledge is manifested in people's behavior, communication, and actions, and it's as complex as human psychology, human culture, and human unpredictability.

In business we think of assets as definite, quantifiable, and concrete. Knowledge assets, though, are much harder to pin down. Is knowledge a process? Is it an object, like a stack of papers? Is it an organic system and emergent from relationships within organizations? Just as a photon can be either a wave or particle, so knowledge can be all these things and more.

When you think of things this way, it should be clear why engaging with the *totality* of your knowledge is so important. If we view knowledge as an absolute truth or a static object, then we're really only seeing it in two dimensions. Engage your intuition, and especially the values that spring from your unconscious, and knowledge appears as something multidimensional—and new and vivid ways of joining the dots between all your knowledge assets will appear to you.

The things we know, and the way we know, lie at the heart of what it is to be human. Knowledge empowers us to reimagine and redefine ourselves and to achieve things that we'd thought impossible. It's through knowledge that we understand our world and extend our capacity to create and innovate; it informs our thoughts and determines the nature and outcome of our actions.

Because knowledge determines the quality of every single action we take, it is critical to learn about and understand what knowledge is so we can be able to use and leverage it in the most efficient and effective ways possible.

See the Whole Picture

Scientists see their disciplines as resting one upon the other. A cognitive psychologist understands that the phenomena they study can also be understood as biological processes; a biologist understands that those processes can be viewed as chemical reactions; a chemist knows that reactions are physical processes; and a physicist recognizes that in the end everything depends upon mathematics.

In the same sort of way, knowledge is composed of different *levels* of understanding. I don't mean the so-called "knowledge pyramid" that you'll sometimes see in old books about knowledge, with raw data at the bottom, information at the midlevel, and "knowledge" at the top. That's an outmoded paradigm: today, we think of knowledge as more like a network, with many different nodes and countless interconnections between them.

LEVEL OF KNOWLEDGE MATURITY	COMPLEXITY OF UNDERSTANDING	TYPE	NOTES
0	None	Data	Raw facts; disorganized and decontextualized
1	Lowest	Information	Organized data based on specific relationships or criteria; the beginnings of interpretation and analysis
2	Low	Know-how	Knowing how things work and how to act
3	Medium	Know-why relating to external world	Knowing why things work the way they do; focusing on the relationships between different elements and underlying patterns
4	Medium-high	Know-why relating to the self	Turning "know-why" inward to learn to question one's biases and trust one's values and intuitions; self-reflection and self-awareness
5	High	Collective wisdom	Knowing the value of others' perspectives; seeing beyond one's own field of vision and using empathy and compassion to unlock a broader view on the VUCA world
6	Highest	Knowledge Mindfulness	Knowledge understood as an interconnected network; the peak of knowledge in action. Seeing the whole and understanding that no single element can work without the others.

When I talk about different levels of understanding, then, I'm really describing the complexity of this system and our ability both to increase the number of nodes comprising the network and to deepen and multiply and strengthen the connections between them. Knowledge, in this sense, is like a living system: the atom gives rise to the molecule, and simple molecules give rise to more complex molecules, and those in turn give rise to compounds and ultimately the biochemical processes we think of as life itself. It's in the connections—in deep complexity and interactions between constituent parts—that the magic happens and through these connections that we arrive at deeper and more meaningful understandings.

These levels are less distinct and rigid than I've made them seem for the purposes of explaining them: they're organic and deeply personal, with each level containing many different shades and internal gradations. As you deepen the complexity of your understanding, you're continuously embedding the insights from the previous levels and relating your new understandings back to those interconnected insights. If my knowledge maturity is at level four, for instance, it means I've added another node to my previous understandings and gained "know-why" insights about myself—personal wisdom!—in addition to know-how and know-why insights about the external world.

In a VUCA world, actively and continuously prioritizing and increasing your knowledge maturity is the only way to succeed. One moves from acquiring data and information that serves the "know-what" into generating meaning in the form of "know-how" and "know-why." This deeper understanding enables us to truly get to the bottom of the problems we're tackling—to address root causes, rather than finding reactive, surface-level fixes that will at best provide only temporary respite.

Many assessments of knowledge stop there, but some take it further. By anchoring knowledge in our own sense of self, our identity, our values and beliefs, it becomes possible to achieve **personal wisdom**—a critical step toward conquering our prejudices and biases and learning to find a deeper purpose that drives us forward even in chaotic and confusing times. If "know-why" stems from focusing on the relationships between apparently fragmented information, and spotting patterns therein, then personal wisdom comes when you begin to reflect deeply on (and connect the dots between) the information within oneself and on oneself as the agent doing the knowing and ask how that shapes and constrains and enables the kind of knowing that you do.

Our increasing personal wisdom flows into and connects with our increasing **collective wisdom** as we begin to realize that our status as the agent of our knowledge, though important, isn't uniquely privileged. What others know is just as important: our own perception is just a single narrow window onto reality, and to truly apprehend the whole—or even come close—is impossible unless we open ourselves to *other* viewpoints and perspectives. Crucially, through this union we gain new ways of viewing not just the problems we're trying to solve, but also ourselves in relation to them: it's often true that you'll see my shortcomings and my potential far more clearly than I'll see them myself.

One common misconception is that the path to knowledge-mindful leadership is an upward spiral: moving from know-how to know-why and onward to personal and collective wisdom. In fact, Knowledge Mindfulness comes when you recognize that all those different elements are part of an integrated whole—a network!—and leverage that understanding to strengthen the connections between them and identify which kinds of knowledge will work best in any given situation. It's when you view knowledge holistically and start seeing the connections and patterns that link all the elements of the whole that you're truly able to act with the conviction and energy needed in today's VUCA world.

The closer we move to Knowledge Mindfulness, the easier it becomes to bring the totality of our interconnected knowledge to bear on the challenges we face in different contexts—to leverage our rational thought *and* our hunches and intuitions and to integrate and elevate the two into something more powerful than either can be on its own. Knowledge-mindful leaders achieve this integration as a byproduct of their commitment to using all the resources at their disposal and to tracing and strengthening the interconnections between them.

The problems of today can't be solved simply by addressing each problem individually or trying to create independent "point solutions" to each new challenge. It's by seeing the connections between all these things that we open up the potential to work with multiple variables and systems simultaneously, driving success in more scalable and efficient ways and unlocking not just new solutions, but radically more effective ways of thinking about the challenges we face.

That's another way of saying that leaders can't operate at the same level of complexity as the problems they're trying to solve. If you're drowning in data, the solution isn't *more* data. Leaders need to consciously work to evolve and enhance the quality and complexity of their knowledge, forge more interconnected and holistic ways of viewing the problems they're facing—then close the loop by ensuring that each new insight elevates their understanding in other areas too. This is Knowledge Mindfulness: the framework that lets us see the interconnections between our knowledge, our self, and the outside world—and consciously leverage those connections to gain higher-quality knowledge; find better, faster, more powerful solutions; and forge a path forward through the VUCA world.

Knowledge and Knowledge Mindfulness

By modern standards early humans lived in comparatively information-poor environments. They had information about the world around them—plants, animals, weather, people—but there were no books or documentaries, no databases or how-to guides, no universities or master classes. That doesn't mean these individuals or their communities were *knowledge* poor, though. Early humans clearly knew a tremendous amount about themselves and the world they inhabited. Knowledge was passed down and preserved through sharing stories, repetition, and oral tradition: for these early communities, the place and power of intuition in processes of knowledge were well understood and routinely leveraged to make sense of and navigate the hostile world around them.

Our failure to "see the whole" and the interconnectedness of our knowledge, our selves, and the broader world—which is to say our failure to be knowledge mindful—leads to serious problems. From physical issues like stress and obesity, to mental problems like anxiety and depression, to moral problems like corruption and violence, to social problems like climate change, the world has become a much more difficult place in which to live. Our ability to survive and thrive in that world is determined by our ability to make sense of and influence our environment and to continually renew our sense of meaning and purpose. That's what Knowledge Mindfulness provides: it's like our life jacket in a stormy sea.

The knowledge-mindful leader knows that to generate the strength and energy required for a VUCA world, we need *all* available resources, and that means drawing together all the fragmented pieces of our knowledge into a unified whole. In a VUCA world, we lack the bandwidth to make sense of the torrents of information in which we swim. We need others to help us, and we need to help others, in order to restore control, find real solutions, and achieve a sense of anchored and holistic meaning.

The American physicist John Archibald Wheeler said, way back in the 1950s, that we live in a "participatory universe." In other words everything we think is real "out there" depends on our beliefs, perceptions, observations, interpretations, and expectations "in here."[23] Your knowledge is uniquely yours; nobody else presented with the same stimuli, the same core facts, would experience them as you do. By the same token, other people *always* have something to add to your knowledge, simply because their own knowledge is uniquely theirs and by definition differs from (and thus can add something to) your own.

Knowledge Mindfulness means learning to engage, expand, and evolve the *totality* of our knowledge—in other words our knowledge maturity—and seeing the whole for what it is, rather than the insufficient fragments that come to us through our rational engagement with the world around us. Our simplest actions convey the essence of all the information we have digested over our lifespan. This process of acquiring and integrating information is something we naturally know how to do, but it's also something that takes a deliberate, continuous, and—yes—*mindful* effort to focus our attention appropriately in a world that's full of distractions. It's all too easy to stop seeking higher understandings and to settle for what you already know (or think you know). That path leads to failure, because unless we consciously and continuously evolve our understandings, we'll get stuck in our comfort zone and never seek to question the stale information, false beliefs, and unexamined biases that surround us.

Knowledge Mindfulness, then, isn't a once-and-done box to be checked off. It's a commitment to thinking actively and strategically about how you relate to and consciously evolve your knowledge and how you can "see" and use knowledge as a cohesive and coherent whole in any given situation. Once you achieve this, you can elevate every aspect of your life. You can take charge of the transformations happening to you and your

> *Unless we consciously and continuously evolve our understandings, we'll get stuck in our comfort zone and never seek to question the stale information, false beliefs, and unexamined biases that surround us.*

environment and restore not only your sense of well-being, but your sense of "well-doing"—your sense that you're not merely drifting but that you're leading with conviction, compassion, and moral clarity.

Knowledge can be thought of as a muscle. By exercising our knowledge—collecting higher-quality and higher-quantity information, integrating what we "think we know" with what we "unthinkingly know," and actively engaging with the holistic knowledge and values of both ourselves and others—we can continuously expand, refresh, and strengthen our knowledge and prepare ourselves to more rapidly and effectively respond to any challenge we face in the future. This isn't just learning; that's just a process of acquiring and building knowledge. Instead, it's *learning and teaching*—giving as much as you take and recognizing that because we're all connected, in helping others you're also helping yourself.

Knowledge can be thought of as falling into different categories, different domains. But the magic happens at the edges—in the liminal spaces where these domains interlock and blur into each other— because that's where exchanges and alchemy can happen and where new ways of knowing arise. Imagine your knowledge as different pools of paint: it's where the colors touch, swirl, and mix that new and beautiful hues arise.

The knowledge-mindful leader knows this and embraces it. Instead of hunkering down, they reach outward. Knowledge is a unique asset in the sense that it appreciates in value the more you leverage it and share it, and it declines in value the more you hoard it away. For leaders, it's our jobs to amplify *all* the different shades of knowledge that exist within our organization and to help our team members and employees to leverage and evolve their knowledge maturity and broaden the totality of their knowledge.

Again, think of Plato's cave. If you just stare at the shadows, you'll have access to only a very limited and misleading stock of knowledge. Knowledge Mindfulness begins with the realization that it's possible to turn to look in the other direction and see the unified truth from which all those apparently disparate and fragmented shadows derived.

The knowledge-mindful leader also knows that reality isn't something to be turned toward and seen in a single flash of insight. Rather, the journey is the destination—there is no absolute truth to be mastered, no single "real" knowledge to be attained. Only through commitment to attaining knowledge maturity and richer meaning— to seeing the whole, uncompromisingly embracing the interplay between different kinds of knowledge, and constantly striving to use the totality of knowledge as it's needed—can we find the best solutions to the challenges we face and learn to lead effectively and efficiently in a VUCA world.

Chapter 3

Understanding Self

Recently, I went to an ABBA concert in London. Surrounded by screaming fans, I watched as Benny, Björn, Agnetha, and Anni-Frid bopped and gyrated their way through the band's greatest hits. It was completely captivating.

But I wasn't *really* watching ABBA at all. I was watching a virtual concert, with holograms and other newfangled technologies used to render the band on stage.

As I sang along to "Dancing Queen," I was struck by the thought that what really made the concert compelling wasn't the technological trickery, nor even the timeless music. It was the energy that every member of the crowd individually brought to the experience: our love of the music, our memories of what the band had meant to us over the years, our emotional investment, and even our intellectual willingness to suspend disbelief and immerse ourselves in the moment.

We're all engaged in a very similar process as we make our way through the world. The things we experience and perceive and respond to aren't fixed and objective—they are impressions and interpretations that depend, in large part, on what we ourselves bring to them. We *construct* the world we live in, drawing not just on what's "out there" but also on what's "in here"—our own past experiences, our beliefs, and our personal and core values. Every moment, in fact, is an act of interpretation; every bit of knowledge depends on how we internalize, process, make sense of, and respond to it.

That's an important insight, because it means that our ability to leverage knowledge and act effectively in the world depends, in large part, on what we ourselves bring to the table. In order to respond in an optimal way to the situations in which we find ourselves, we need to start by looking inward—so we can understand the processes that shape not only *how* we see and understand the world but also *where* we put our attention and focus and start to take control over the processes of judgment, intuition, and insight that ultimately enable us to take smarter, more effective actions.

We'll delve more fully into the way we relate to the world around us—including the organizations we lead!—in the next chapter. For now, though, I want to dig more deeply into the ways in which, by elevating our own self-knowledge (which is to say, our own role as agents of knowledge), we can optimize and evolve the way we generate, share, and use knowledge in our lives and in our leadership.

That starts with recognizing that what we think of as "our self" isn't really a single unitary thing. It's a *living system* of densely inter-connected processes through which knowledge flows. What's more, it isn't a static system: it's a dynamic and organic one. That means some aspects of our "self" can be perceived as constructions, developed over time, and shaped by the experiences and accumulated knowledge we acquire as we live and grow in the world.

In the last chapter, we learned about the totality of our knowledge and how leveraging the entirety of our knowledge can elevate our ability to operate effectively in the world both as individuals and as leaders. In this chapter we'll learn about the totality of our*selves* and about the way that our knowledge stems not just from "out there," but also from what happens within us—not just the thoughts in our head, but all the different dimensions that make up the full spectrum of our knowing and thus our being.

It's by embracing ourselves holistically, I'll argue, that we can arrive at an expanded understanding of what we ourselves can be and do in the world. This is an urgent insight for leaders in today's troubled world—because only by expanding our understanding of ourselves (and being mindful of the way our "self" relates to other elements of the Knowledge Mindfulness framework) can we relate effectively to others and truly develop our ability to live, love, and lead in more productive and compassionate ways.

The Totality of Self

Who are you? It's a simple-sounding question, but not one you can answer simply by showing your business card or even by looking in the mirror. Your sense of self is necessarily multidimensional: I'm a partner *and* a mom *and* a researcher *and* an author *and* a businesswoman. We contain multitudes—some complementary, some contradictory, and all important parts of who we are.

More than just the different roles we play in our lives, though, our selves are multidimensional because they are composed of different, yet integrated, dimensions. If you look at the book in your hands, you can understand it on multiple levels: the physics of the quarks and

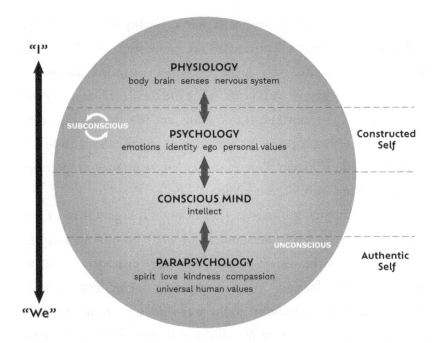

atoms and molecules that make it up, the chemistry of ink on paper, the economics of book publishing, or the meaning of the words you're reading. In just the same way, we need to think through the different levels on which our selves exist and can be understood.

These levels aren't actually distinct, of course. The layers I'm outlining are descriptive, not structural: they're there to help us to understand but don't reflect actual boundaries in how we're built. We're much more organic and intermingled than that—but sometimes we need to create categories and distinctions in order to perceive the interconnections more clearly.

Let's start with the most tangible and obvious level: that of **physiology**. Our bodies and physical sensations are a key part of what makes us the people we are. The signals we receive from our nervous systems and our five senses are critical precursors to virtually everything else about us.

Now imagine you're stepping a little deeper, into the level of **psychology**, where subconscious emotional signals rise up in reaction to the sensory information mediated by our conscious experiences. Psychology thus comprises what we often (mistakenly!) think of as the sum total of our interior lives: not just reflexive responses to pleasure and pain, but more meaningful emotional responses, personal values, ego, and identity.

Beyond this lies our **conscious mind**, where we process sensory information and emotional responses into rational thought and intellect. It's here that the signals from our senses, having been received and interpreted by the brain, produce a subset of our knowledge. The conscious mind also feeds into the subconscious (and vice versa, of course), which serves as a kind of shortcut to speed our access to the learnings and memories we've rehearsed and deeply internalized.

Finally, deepest of all, lies the realm of **parapsychology**. By parapsychology I don't mean telepathy or the ability to talk to ghosts—I mean the deep-seated spiritual and human values that truly define who we are. These values, bubbling up from our unconscious, are the bedrock of ourselves, and engaging with and leveraging them effectively is a critical part of the dynamics of Knowledge Mindfulness.

It's important to understand, here, that these "layers" are actually parts of a dynamic system. We don't sit back passively and let knowledge move inward through sensory signals, then percolate down through our psychology, our consciousness, and further downward. The reality is much more active—something closer to what Augustine meant when he wrote of perception as being "the soul's attention ... striving to reach out and sense things through the flesh."[24]

Our "selves," seen in this way, are a fusion of inward motions of sensory inputs, but also (in my view) of multiple active processes of outreach, interpretation, and integration. Each layer both gives and takes, shapes and is shaped, as part of an energetic and deeply active process—construction and deconstruction, questioning and reinforcing—that determines both the knowledge available to us and the actions we are able to take in the world. As knowledge-mindful leaders, we need to understand and leverage these processes, with deep understanding and active self-awareness, in order to unlock our own potential and lead our organizations forward more effectively and successfully.

The Constructed Self

My kids used to love a Japanese video game called *Katamari Damacy*, in which—for no clear reason—the player is expected to roll a small, sticky ball around the playing field, hoovering up everything they pass and gradually getting bigger and bigger over time. First, the player starts with thumbtacks and shrubs; eventually, they move on to absorbing trucks, buildings, and even mountains, dragging everything they encounter along with them as they grow.

In much the same way, most of what we think of as our "self" is the result of the knowledge and experience we accumulate over time. We're natural absorbers of information: from the "blooming, buzzing confusion" of infancy, we gradually learn and internalize more and more about the world around us. It's from these experiences—starting with our senses, moving through our feelings, and becoming part of what we think of as our conscious or rational mind—that much of what we think of as ourselves is built.

It's important to realize, though, that this accumulation is precisely that: not something we inherently *are*, not a product, but rather a dynamic construct that affects and is affected by its interaction with the external world around it. This is what the Sufi scholar Kabir Edmund Helminski calls our "artificial self-construct," which he sees as born of "social programming and conditioning."[25] That doesn't make the constructed self less real, but it does make it less foundational: it's something we can mold, shape, and build, rather than something we build upon.

Critically, this artificial self is where many of the things we consider negative about ourselves can be found. Our compulsions and fears, our selfishness and pride, our likes and dislikes, our defense mechanisms and our judgmentalism, and even our preoccupations and expectations—all these things are products of our ever-changing experiences of the world, from early childhood memories and cultural socialization to the experiences and learnings we gather to us over time.

Many of the things we consider our personal values also spring up from this part of our selves. I might want to get a promotion, become incredibly wealthy, or write a bestseller—but these goals are rooted in short-lived, short-term values that themselves spring from my past experiences and traumas. These constructions aren't inherently bad or worthless: they're the things that motivate and drive us through life, after all! But their lifespan is very short, and they are only a part of what makes us who we are. For longer-term and more purposeful and fulfilling motivators, we need to tap into and expand our cognition by bringing it into contact with the *unconscious* self—the "authentic self" where our deepest and most universal human values lie.

It's important to recognize here that our constructed selves aren't *bad* or *negative*. The constructed self is a dynamic system that mediates our relationship with the world around us, serving as both bridge and buffer. It shapes and filters our insights and our perceptions both of the world and of ourselves; it is, in this sense, a tool that can be used to either positive or negative effect, depending largely on the extent of our self-knowledge.

For longer-term and more purposeful and fulfilling motivators, we need to tap into and expand our cognition by bringing it into contact with the unconscious self—the "authentic self."

The key, as with any tool, is to understand and use our constructed selves mindfully. It's when we fail to recognize the agency we have in shaping our constructed selves, or mistake constructed interpretations for inherent aspects of ourselves or the world around us, that we run into trouble. If we can elevate our awareness of these aspects and tame, manage, or redirect them, it becomes possible to take things that once seemed negative and transform them into much more positive and fruitful aspects of our inner lives.

Finding the Authentic Self

Helminski sees the self as existing on a kind of spectrum. "At one end is the false and artificial self-construct of the person who has not known him- or herself, who has not made the inner journey of self-knowledge," he writes. "At the other end of the spectrum is a more natural, spontaneous self without artifice. As we become relatively free of the identification with our social programming and conditioning, we come to know the purified subjectivity or awareness that is our innate nature." It's by striving for and reaching for this deeper, more authentic self, he argues, that we can unlock our spiritual nature "including the capacity for conscious choice, unconditional love, and fundamental creativity."[26]

This "essential" self exists in the area of parapsychology: the science of studying the spirit. It's here that we can access the foundational human values that truly make us who we are. If fear and falsehood spring from (or grow embedded in) the constructed self, by accessing the authentic self, we can find a pathway to creativity, joy, and a deep and lasting inner peace, even amid the tumult of the VUCA world.

There are parallels here to the concept of quantum consciousness. We all know that classical physics falls short when confronted with certain kinds of phenomena, and one of the toughest nuts to crack is explaining the way our minds work, how two pounds of spongy gray matter can give rise to all the wonders of our conscious experiences. One possible explanation is that the strange and (to quote Einstein) "spooky" properties of quantum particles might serve as a kind of bridge to a radically different way of understanding the foundation of our conscious experience.

But you don't have to dismantle conventional physics to recognize that we all have a kind of spiritual DNA and that there are things about who we are that are so deep-seated that they're effectively encoded in our spiritual selves. Accessing and understanding these deep values is critical, because unlike the constructed self, the authentic self truly is foundational. It's the basis of who we are—it's where our intentions are conceived, directing our attention and consequently our action. It's when we ignore that, or when our constructed and artificial selves fall out of synchronization, that real problems start to arise. We need to do the work of fully knowing ourselves in order to overcome the gravitational pull of our constructed selves.

This happens at the level of the organization, too, of course. The environmentalist and economist Paul Hawken argues that "the ultimate purpose of business is not, or should not be, simply to make money. Nor is it merely a system of making and selling things. The promise of business is to increase the general well-being of humankind through service, a creative invention and ethical philosophy."[27] What Hawken describes corresponds, in a way, to the spiritual dimension we trace in our own selves—it's the authentic purpose of the organization, which itself necessarily reflects the authentic selves and spiritual values of the leaders and employees who make up that organization.

As knowledge-mindful leaders, we have two main tasks: to elevate our knowledge maturity by becoming personally wiser and more aware of the multidimensional nature of self and the interconnections between those dimensions and the context within which we operate and to lead others toward that same knowledge maturity in order to unlock collective wisdom. In order to achieve that, we first need to understand the way that our authentic selves connect with our constructed selves and thereby with the world around us.

Our values, our spiritual dimension, are the missing piece of the puzzle without which nothing else makes sense. As leaders we need to find that missing piece and help our teams to find their own missing pieces too—and to recognize how all those interconnected pieces fit together, so we can creatively and effectively leverage all the different pieces at our disposal—in order to find a path to centeredness and joyful purpose, even amid the destabilizing chaos of the VUCA world.

Look Inward as well as Outward

Now, in this chapter I've worked to decompose the self into its constituent parts, then to systematically describe how all these parts relate to one another. I've even shown you a diagram setting it all down in black and white. Only one problem: it doesn't actually work that way at all!

I've shown the self as a collection of parts in order to simplify and explain it to you—but the reality is that the self *isn't* really fragmented. Your physiological and psychological and parapsychological functions aren't distinct and static and neatly layered, like geological strata. They're far more fluid than that, and they're constantly interacting and influencing one another.

It's important to realize that there are some parts of our self that are flexible and changeable—like our sense of identity, our feelings, and our ego—and others that are fixed and foundational (and, often, largely neglected) such as our spiritual bedrock. It's by understanding this and seeking to approach a more holistic view of ourselves that we can learn to change that which can be changed, learn to respect and draw upon that which is fixed and enduring, and learn to be mindful in distinguishing between the two.

Once we have a more elevated and all-encompassing understanding of our self, we can start to recognize it as a source of information. Far too often we see the world "out there"—reaching us through our five senses—as the entirety of our world. But the reality is that information flows in both directions: into us, from the world, to be digested by our rational mind; but also upward and outward, *from within us*, as we tap into our own psychology and deepest-rooted and most enduring spiritual qualities and decide what to focus on, attend to, and draw toward us.

It's useful, here, to turn to the work of Ervin Laszlo, who has done so much to theorize and popularize the concept of quantum consciousness. In his excellent book *The Self-Actualizing Cosmos*, Laszlo writes, "It appears that two forms of reception of information from the world are available to the brain, and not just one. In addition to perceiving the world through the bodily sense organs, the brain can perceive some elements of the world nonlocally, through quantum decoding."[28]

Similarly, Laszlo notes, the psychiatrist Stanislav Grof argues that "we can obtain information about the universe in two radically different ways. Besides the conventional possibility of learning through sensory perception, and analysis and synthesis of the data, we can also find out about various aspects of the world by direct identification with them in altered states of consciousness."

Now, we don't need to delve into the details of "quantum decoding" or "altered states of consciousness" to recognize that Laszlo and Grof have struck on something profound: the critical insight that our senses are not the *only* source of the things we know. The totality of knowledge, in this sense, means recognizing that both of these sources—knowledge from outside and knowledge from deep within—are valid and valuable and using them to strengthen and support one another.

Knowledge Mindfulness helps us understand these interconnections and realize the totality of our knowledge. In doing so one of our main objectives is precisely this: to improve our sensitivity to and awareness of *all* the signals and information flowing through us. By elevating our understanding and awareness of these interconnections, we can unlock new dimensions of ourselves—new pathways of knowledge!—that we never previously attended to or even realized existed.

In elevating our self-knowledge, we also increase our knowledge maturity to the level of personal wisdom—a word that really means our ability to exercise good judgment and perceive things clearly without being pulled off course by biases, egotism, identity, and untested beliefs. Wisdom means focusing our *attention* on the things that really matter—and thereby leveraging its connection to our *intention*—which is another way of saying our soul or our spiritual dimension.

We seldom really examine the power of attention—we don't attend to our attention! But while attention might seem invisible or insignificant, it's really evident everywhere we look. Everything humanity has created sprang, in the first instance, from this interplay between "attention" and "intention"—it's the *primum mobile* that breathes life and momentum into everything we do as individuals, as organizations, and as a species. This spark is present in companies, too, of course: it shapes corporate cultures, giving them a sense of identity that serves as the central attractor for the complex system of relationships that make up an enterprise.

To take just one example, our psychology—our emotions, our identity, and our ego—plays a key role in mediating our ability to acquire external information and build knowledge. Our biases and incorrect assumptions act as a barrier, preventing information from coming in and creating blind spots that prevent leaders from quickly and accurately perceiving the events going on around them—especially during times of stress or crisis. When we feel overburdened, we're more likely to filter out information that doesn't agree with our preconceptions—unless we're aware of that risk and work from a place of Knowledge Mindfulness to change the dynamic by integrating psychological factors into a broader and more holistic totality of knowledge.

In a similar vein, our feelings and emotions typically operate much faster than conscious thought, which is what makes subconscious, emotionally mediated processes so important and powerful. But it's by understanding our feelings, and where they come from, in a conscious way that we can begin to gain conscious insights into and control over those subconscious processes and learn to leverage them more mindfully. It's by embracing and learning to understand the *connectedness* of ourselves, in other words, that we can truly expand the possibilities of our knowledge.

And, of course, ego and emotions are just a couple of aspects of our inner self. The more we evolve the totality of our knowledge, the more we can evolve our "self," too, and use more of our full potential as we relate to and forge new connections with the world around us. When we act with a holistic sense of self, we are able to draw upon our deepest spiritual traits; refine, restrain, or reevaluate our changeable constructed qualities; and find richer, more ennobling, and more effective ways of relating both to ourselves and to our place in the world around us.

In Search of Harmony

As knowledge-mindful leaders, we need to use this evolved sense of self—integrated, inward and outward looking, holistic—to develop knowledge maturity that lets us pull free of our own uninspected biases and rise above our fears and doubts. By clarifying our own sense of self, we can help those around us—our employees, our peers, and so forth—to find clarity of their own and elevate the performance of our entire organization.

To achieve this harmonious, holistic sense of self, we need to acknowledge and understand the interconnections between the different dimensions of our selves. The most common error that we make in attempting (or failing) to do this is a kind of category error: we assume that *all* aspects of our selves are foundational and authentic, when in fact many are constructed and artificial. That's a big problem, because when we perceive something as foundational, we stop trying to question, challenge, or change it.

A bias or preference, for instance, can be a useful thing: it is a heuristic that lets you make decisions and operate effectively in the world. I know I prefer chocolate ice cream, and that means I don't need to try every single flavor in the store when I'm deciding which one to buy. If you sell paper, you might know from experience that people generally want more paper during a given season and increase your on-hand inventory accordingly, even if you haven't yet started to see an uptick in orders.

But if you believe your biases and preferences are foundational—part of *who you are* or part of *how the world is*—then things get much more problematic. It's what might lead a paper business to keep doubling down on increasing inventory even as people are switching to another supplier or moving toward digital tools instead. More broadly this process is also how racism and partisanship grow entrenched in our societies and how we wind up in places where it's impossible to compromise or find a path to progress.

> *We assume that* all *aspects of our selves are foundational and authentic, when in fact many are constructed and artificial.*

It's also how we can grow unhappy and alienated from ourselves. If my authentic self is anchored in kindness and compassion, but I've somehow developed constructed values of selfishness and bitterness, then I will feel deeply unhappy as I move through the world. Today's surging mental health crisis is due, at least in part, to precisely this kind of conflict and disconnection: the more we lose sight of our authentic selves and the more we come to mistake our constructed selves for our authentic selves, the harder it becomes to live without sadness, confusion, and instability.

This happens in the business world, too, of course. As individual leaders and workers, we're experiencing soaring rates of burnout, in large part because our values and sense of purpose have grown disconnected from the reality of the VUCA world. Without authentic values to guide us through that fog—or leaders capable of communicating those authentic values across their organization—that sense of malaise will only grow in the months and years to come.

What's needed is a much deeper understanding of ourselves—to pull us out of that confusion or to stop us from ever descending into it. The more you understand yourself—and your feelings, your triggers, your personal beliefs, and your deep values—the better you are able to manage the situations in which you find yourself. By understanding *both* your artificial and authentic selves, you will be able to ask, why am I doing the things I'm doing? Am I being driven by artificial beliefs or by the things I know to be truly right for me and for those around me? And how can I best lean into my authentic values to deliver the kind of leadership my organization and my employees need during these challenging times?

In *The Tao of Physics*, the American physicist Fritjof Capra argues that science and spirituality are two sides of the same coin—opposing, in some senses, but also deeply connected. To exist peacefully and purposefully in the world, he argues, it's necessary to delve into both worlds—to see *both* sides of the coin. "To paraphrase an old Chinese saying, mystics understand the roots of the Tao but not its branches; scientists understand its branches but not its roots. Science does not need mysticism and mysticism does not need science; but men and women need both," he writes.[29]

In much the same way, we need to learn to see the totality of ourselves: to recognize and distinguish the constructed and the authentic and to use both in harmony in order to elevate and evolve the way we "see" and use knowledge, the way we lead, and even the way we exist in the world.

From "I" to "We"

In her excellent book *Thrivability*, Jean M. Russell notes that we're frequently mistaken about the things we think will make us happy.[30] Studies show that people who win the lottery and people who have terrible accidents that leave them unable to walk are equally happy one year after the incident. In other words neither sudden wealth nor sudden disability actually impacts the level of happiness we feel.

That's an extraordinary insight that shows how much of our well-being is actually anchored not in superficial wants or beliefs, but in deeper values such as love and compassion. This is reflected not just in a deepening of the values themselves, but in a change in their fundamental quality: in our constructed selves, we tend to focus on ourselves and our own wants and needs—from sensations like hunger, to feelings like pleasure or fear, to beliefs and desires such as wanting wealth or power. In our authentic selves, however, universal values such as love and compassion come to the fore—and it's by honoring and making space for those values that we find real and lasting peace, happiness, and joy.

In the diagram at the start of this chapter, you'll see this represented by the arrow on the left-hand side: at the surface our social programming and ego drive us to focus on "I" and "me," while as we move deeper we find ourselves increasingly able to think in terms of "we" or "us."

This isn't just about the difference between selfishness and selflessness. It's also about a fundamental shift in mindset about how we relate to the world. As the Dalai Lama writes, "How people treat their fellow human beings and the world around them largely depends on how they conceive of themselves."[31] When you see the world in terms of "I" or "me," your focus is on differences: *I want this* so *you can't have it.* Or *I am one thing* and *you are something else.* This, quite naturally, puts us on a path to conflict and isolation; it's inherently a zero-sum way of viewing the world.

Find your way to a "we" mindset, and things look very different. Instead of differences it becomes possible to see similarities and commonalities—to find pathways to interconnectedness, rather than simply pushing people away. When you embrace your deepest values, you come to see that you aren't the center of the universe—and that makes it possible to forge strong connections with others and lean into values such as care, compassion, and love.

For leaders that's essential because if we can't understand and connect with others, we can't influence them or engage them in processes of collaboration and cocreation. A knowledge-mindful leader who appreciates the importance of the "we" mindset will be able to communicate more effectively, coordinate change efforts more successfully, and draw out the creative talents of others.

This might sound a bit fluffy, especially for a book that's designed to help business leaders. But careful! That's your constructed self talking. Research shows that while we might *think* we're designed to be selfish and self-serving, on a deeper level we're actually built for compassion. Unlike those of most other animals, the human brain is packed with mirror neurons that fire when we watch someone else acting.

The psychiatrist and psychoanalyst Daniel Stern suggests that these neurons are tasked with enabling "the participation in another's mental life" and the ability to share in the intentions and feelings of those around us.[32] At the most basic level, then, our brains are hardwired for empathy and for connecting with and trying to understand and emulate the behavior and feelings of those around us.

Researchers believe that compassion and altruism are evolved traits. Darwin argued that groups whose members cooperated and helped one another "would flourish best, and rear the greatest number of offspring."[33] More recently it's been argued that individuals who look outward, help others, and operate from a place of deep values are likely to be more collaborative, more trustworthy, and more likely to spark mutually beneficial exchanges with others—so, traits such as compassion and kindness are actually much "better" for us as individuals than traits such as selfishness, fearfulness, and suspicion.

For thinkers like Ervin Laszlo, this relates to the insight that just as every living organism fundamentally seeks "coherence"—the maintenance of its own system, in its totality, as a living whole—so too every living organism depends upon its coherence in relation to *other* organisms. "Coherence does not stop at the individual," Laszlo writes in *The Self-Actualizing Cosmos*. "Viable organisms in the biosphere are both individually and collectively coherent. They are *supercoherent* . . . Any species, ecology, or individual that is not coherent in itself and is not coherently related to other species and ecologies is disadvantaged in its reproductive strategies. It becomes marginalized and ultimately dies out, eliminated by the merciless workings of natural selection."[34]

Humans, Laszlo notes, have considered themselves the exception to this rule, because they are able to use technology to overcome the ecological shortcomings that follow as supercoherence breaks down. Increasingly, though, we're seeing that such "solutions" are really just Band-Aids. As leaders in a VUCA world, we need to recommit to building coherence across all our networks of operation—and that means fully embracing the "we" mindset.

The bottom line is that the more we understand ourselves and understand our knowledge in relation to the totality of our knowledge and in relation to our ability to lead people and organizations, the more we find ourselves also turning toward others. "We" is always stronger than "me"—and it's by deepening our understanding of ourselves and embracing and activating our core human values that we can access this kind of connected and compassionate way of operating in the world both as individuals and as leaders.

The Self in the World

As leaders we can't control or manage complex systems directly. We can only really manage our own selves—and, through that, the roles, relationships, and activities that define how we participate in the systems of which we're part. Still, that makes it doubly important to understand the dynamics of these complex systems—because the better we understand them and see the connections that shape their operations, the more we'll be able to take actions that serve us while also supporting the health and vitality of the whole.

Knowledge-mindful leaders are highly astute and self-aware. They recognize the value of their constructed selves. But they also work to integrate (and, when necessary, reconfigure) *all* their different layers in order to increase the quality of their knowledge, the quality of their perception, and ultimately the quality of their actions. This is what's meant by achieving harmony. The knowledge-mindful leader still relies on their feelings, beliefs, and rational thought in order to lead, of course. But they ensure their artificial or constructed aspects are firmly anchored in their foundational and authentic selves, enabling them to act and lead with far more clarity and conviction.

If you came to this book looking for new or better-quality kinds of knowledge, congratulations! In understanding yourself you can unlock a true unrealized source of knowledge—and in understanding how your self relates to the totality of your knowledge and to the world around you, you can enrich your experiences, and thus your life, and dramatically expand the possibilities open to you as a person, as a leader, and as an actor navigating and seeking to help others to thrive in the VUCA world.

You can also lean into this understanding to get more from those around you. Everyone's unique blend of constructed selves gives rise to new perspectives and insights on the world around them, like light refracting into countless different colors. Knowledge Mindfulness helps you to recognize and leverage that fact, opening your mind to others and honoring their own feelings and interpretations of reality while remaining secure in your own authentic self and core values.

As Daniel Goleman has noted, empathy and compassion—the ability to think in terms of "we" rather than "me"—is a vital skill for business leaders.[35] When you lead with empathy, you can get along with (and get the best out of) others, and you can learn to see the world through the eyes of those around you in order to gain new insights and discover new possibilities.

Again: this isn't just fluff! Research shows that empathy, and the ability to mentally open yourselves to different perspectives, directly correlates to leaders' performance and thus to organizational performance. If you want your company to succeed, you need to start by understanding yourself in a deep and meaningful way—and then use that understanding to change how you relate to your employees, your customers, and the world around you.

> *Everyone's unique blend of constructed selves gives rise to new perspectives and insights on the world around them, like light refracting into countless different colors.*

To understand how that works in practice, we need to think about how the self interfaces with the external world, and vice versa—and how leaders can leverage that to lead their organizations forward. That's what we'll turn to in the next chapter.

Chapter 4

Understanding the External World

Business leaders are smart people, and that can be dangerous. Here's what Rumi, the Sufi mystic, has to say about it:

Yesterday I was clever, so I wanted to change the world.
Today, I am wise, so I am changing myself.

Now, Rumi isn't saying we should simply accept the world as it is and bend ourselves out of shape in order to fit in. What he's saying, I think, is that if you simply wade into the world and start trying to change things, you won't get anywhere. Any attempt to change the world—or lead an organization—needs to start with a process of mindful self-examination, because everything about your interaction with the world depends on your understanding of the relationship between you and the world.

In the last chapter, we explored what it means—for you, your leadership, and your organization—to understand the totality of one's self. In this chapter, I want to ask how that self connects with the world: what are the relationships that mediate our existence in a confusing and complex world? What are we affected by, and what effects do we have on others? It's by understanding these interconnections on a deep level, I'd argue, that we are able to shape the organizations around us and to leverage the *totality* of our selves and all the other insights that Knowledge Mindfulness brings in order to bring out the best in our organizations and in those around us.

That's an important question, because as we all know, living and leading in a VUCA world can be a traumatizing experience. The world around is confusing, fast changing, and hard to make sense of—and yet we are expected to do our jobs, support our families, lead our organizations forward, and take responsibility for the apparently impossible task of achieving clarity and certainty amid the noise and chaos. It's hardly surprising that we're seeing such high rates of executive burnout or that so many of our employees are suffering from poor morale and even mental health challenges.

What most people don't realize is that the trauma of the VUCA world really springs from our lack of knowledge about *how* to act effectively. All the traits of the VUCA world—volatility, uncertainty, confusion, and ambiguity—are really different ways of describing a state of ignorance about how the world is today and how it will be tomorrow. It's our *lack of knowledge* about the world we live in, and about our place in it, that causes us so much pain.

Worst of all, our response to this pain is to recoil and hunker down. When we can't make sense of the world around us, we retreat inward: ignorance leads us to fear those around us, which in turn creates mistrust. We withdraw into fragile certainties, such as prejudices and biases, that tell us it's okay to stop even trying to test or validate our ideas against the outside world.

That's a dangerous place to inhabit. Taken to an extreme, it leads us to what the South African philosopher John McDowell, in his book *Mind and World*, memorably termed "frictionless spinning in a void"—existing in a state of absolute isolation from the world, from the context we inhabit, and from the people around us.[36] And of course, the less connected we are to the world, the less sense the world makes to us. We're left with a cycle in which complexity leads to ignorance, ignorance leads to isolation—and isolation exacerbates our sense of the world's incomprehensible complexity.

On an individual level, this cycle all too easily leads to angst and alienation. On a societal level, it leads to dangerous levels of extremism and intractable partisanship. And on an organizational level, it leads to a deep breakdown of the communication, collaboration, and cohesion that are required to tackle the challenges of the VUCA world.

As Rumi realized, we can't solve that problem simply by seeking to impose our will on the world around us. That leads to frustration and failure. But as leaders we need to find a way to break this cycle—to fight the tendency to withdraw and instead to forge stronger connections to the world around us.

In this chapter I'll ask you to consider that the solution lies not just in *having* knowledge or *using* knowledge, but in *situating* our knowledge in a meaningful context. Being clever is great, but we need to be wise too!

By embracing Knowledge Mindfulness, I'll argue, it's possible to unlock connections that were previously unseen or out of reach and to leverage them to create a far more integrated and holistically anchored way of existing in the world. Through doing so it's possible to choose a better path forward—in our communication, in our behavior, and in our decisions—to drive success for ourselves and our organizations.

We have already seen the importance of looking inward and understanding the totality of our selves. Now it's time to step up and recognize that leadership also means looking out at the different ecosystems of which we're part—not just the natural environment, but also our families, our organizations, our communities, our nations, and even the planet we share. It's by bringing the totality of our self-knowledge into connection with these ecosystems, and using it to create thriving environments in which our teams can unlock the totality of *their* self-knowledge, that we can come together to flourish and drive success for ourselves and others.

Why Context Matters

When people ask me why context is so important, I like to tell a story about a sports car.

Imagine the car of your dreams—a Lamborghini, say. Imagine the glittering paint job, the roaring engine, the amazing feeling of sitting behind the wheel. Think about all the hundreds of hours of research and craftsmanship that went into making that car possible and the hours you yourself spent learning to drive and studying every part of the vehicle. Imagine the thrill of putting the pedal to the metal and roaring confidently along a highway at a hundred miles an hour.

Now imagine that the windows suddenly turn black and that you can't see anything around you. You're still behind the wheel of an amazing, finely tuned machine, but suddenly it isn't thrilling to be racing along a highway—it's terrifying!

That's the situation that leaders are in today if they understand their own processes of knowledge but lack awareness and insight into the *context* of the situation they are in. It doesn't matter how powerful or capable or intelligent you are as an individual—if you can't connect your processes of knowledge to the world around you, you're heading for an unpleasant crash.

When it comes to knowledge, after all, context is everything. That's because knowledge is purposeful—the chaotic signals coming in from the outside world have to be prioritized and sorted, attended to and analyzed, and marshaled toward a clear goal in order to become knowledge. Whether our knowledge travels inward via our senses or bubbles up directly from our core values, we can only make sense of it if we know where we stand in relation to everything else.

As I said previously, it's a bit like Archimedes and his lever: give me a long enough rod and a firm place to stand, the Greek said, and I'll change the world. Knowledge is the lever, but you still need a firm foundation—a solid and purposeful place to stand, relative to everything else in the world—in order to make use of that lever.

In a VUCA world, though, finding that firm place to stand— that sense not just of who you are, but of who you are in relation to everything else—can be tough. Every change or development in both the external environment and your internal self creates new signals and messages that we need to attend to—some weak and some strong; some obscure or confusing and some clear as a bell; some authentic and meaningful and others spurious or misleading.

We're constantly bombarded by these signals, and the more signals that flood in, the harder it becomes to make sense of them and organize them—or determine how to prioritize them and where to direct our attention and our focus. In this our sense of purpose is like a magnet that draws in only the signals that matter most to us in any given moment and excludes the rest. When you're thinking about knowledge, in other words, *what* you want to know is shaped in large part by *why* you're seeking knowledge in the first place.

This, of course, is why the cycle of ignorance and alienation is so toxic: the more you withdraw from the world, the narrower your sense of purpose becomes and the less you'll seek signals that might challenge or expand your perspective. Instead of evolving you'll grow entrenched in a self-perpetuating cycle of insularity.

What might be less immediately apparent, though, is that this insight is also critically important for leaders and their organizations. As leaders our sense of ourselves—our sense of identity, which stems from self-knowledge—plays a critical role in determining how we relate to the world around us, from our direct reports to our organization as a whole and from our customers to our competitors.

As leaders, too, we have a critical role to play in shaping our organization's sense of itself and creating an organizational identity that reflects the shared values and vision that we all aspire to. The mental image we have of our organization, and the metaphors we use to organize and guide it, will directly impact the way that our organization understands the context in which it operates and the way in which we onboard, sort, and use knowledge across our operations.

From Machines to Living Systems

If I ask how you think of your organization, you might tell me, we sell such-and-such a product, or offer such-and-such a service, or serve this or that kind of customer. Fair enough. But that kind of answer really addresses what a company *does*, not what it *is*.

As leaders we need to know what our company does, of course. But we also need a clear image of how our organization operates—

the guiding principles or operating metaphor that shapes its culture, explains how its different parts interact, and determines how we ourselves need to act in order to get the best out of it.

Only one problem: the explanations of these principles that you'll typically hear if you visit a business school or a boardroom are horribly ill suited to the reality of the VUCA world.

The problem dates way back to 1909, when the mechanical engineer Frederick Winslow Taylor—a pioneer of industrial efficiency who went on to become one of the first management consultants—published *The Principles of Scientific Management.*[37] In his pioneering book, Taylor set out the idea that a workplace was effectively a machine and could be optimized and operated by treating people in much the same way as pistons and pinwheels.

Though it's drawn a great deal of criticism over the years—including being parodied by everyone from Aldous Huxley to Charlie Chaplin—the central tenets of Taylorism remain deeply anchored in today's corporate culture. When you see a company like Amazon "optimizing" its workers to breaking point or firms using "rank-and-yank" methods to weed out underperforming employees, you're seeing the enduring power of the notion that companies and their people are like machines.

There are plenty of problems with that concept, of course. But from the standpoint of Knowledge Mindfulness, the "machine metaphor" is especially toxic because it suggests that the leader's role is simply to push a button and let the machine run on the tracks laid out for it. There's no room, in this worldview, for individual employees to have opinions or insights; there's no room for challenging or questioning assumptions; there's no room for evolution or change, but merely a static framework and the relentless pursuit of efficiency.

A Taylorist leader sees their entire organization as a single fixed system. They might make tweaks here or there to try to eke out a bit of additional mechanical advantage, but in principle everything is fixed in place. That might be okay if the company is already basically on the right track and nothing needs changing—but in a VUCA world, we need to be far more agile and adaptive. We need to be able to lead our companies in *new* directions and unlock the creativity and insight of our employees in order to overcome unprecedented challenges.

To achieve that we need a *new* operating metaphor. The knowledge-mindful leader recognizes that the world—and the organization—is much more complex and interesting than Taylor imagined. They see the organization not merely as a mechanical system, but rather as a *living* system: messy, organic, ever-changing, and comprising systems of knowledge expressed through networks of connected individuals, who are in turn part of a larger and densely interconnected ecosystem.

When your mental image tells you that your organization is a living system, rather than a machine, a number of important things change. First of all you perceive your organization as fundamentally human centered. People aren't just interchangeable cogs—they are individuals with their own profoundly important perspectives and insights on the challenges your business faces.

Crucially, too, those people aren't operating in isolation. It's the connections between them—not org charts and hierarchies, but shifting social ties and emergent webs of organic networks of knowledge sharing and knowledge generation—that truly transform the organization into a living system. This is a point that Arie de Geus, the Royal Dutch Shell executive, makes extraordinarily well: "Companies can learn because they are living beings," he writes in *The*

Living Company. "If they were mere 'bundles of assets,' they would be dead objects, and learning would be impossible for them."[38]

Because of this, when you view your organization as a living system, your own self-image changes. For a leader your job is no longer simply to blow the whistle or pull the lever that fires up the machine you've built. Instead, your job is to nurture the entire living system, by nurturing in turn the informal networks where communication and connection happen. Your job isn't simply to issue directives—it's to cultivate your own presence in ways that benefit the entire ecosystem and create an environment in which your organization, and its knowledge, can thrive.

The Window to Collective Wisdom

Part of the process of cultivating your organization's connections is to recognize that there is no single system that comprises your organization. Your organization is part of a bigger system (or ecosystem) of other organizations, which in turn is part of a regionally and ultimately globally connected series of *other* macrosystems. And your organization is *made up* of systems, too, starting with its interconnected functional divisions and communities of practice and moving down to individuals who are themselves (as we saw in the previous chapter) made up of dynamic systems of knowledge.

The knowledge-mindful leader understands this and constantly strives to see themselves and their organization as part of a dynamic, mutually dependent network of microsystems and macrosystems, both larger and smaller. As Verna Allee argues, businesses "are evolving into the networked patterns of living systems," and leaders, in turn, are having to learn new ways of managing knowledge across their organizations. Viewing businesses as living systems isn't just a metaphor; it's a practical necessity in the tumultuous world we now share and also a deeply practical insight that can guide us toward new ways of managing and leading. "We have mastered engineering and reengineering, but living systems require a different mindset and completely different management tools," Allee writes.[39]

One insight that comes when you recognize that, as a leader, you are caring for a living system is that it becomes more important to follow the principle every junior doctor learns: *first, do no harm.* Our decisions, as leaders, grow more consequential—our *responsibilities* are greater—when we recognize our stewardship of a living ecosystem.

Fortunately, as knowledge-mindful leaders, we also have the tools to grow into this new role. In leveraging the collective wisdom of our teams and our organizations, we turn each of our personal connections into a sensor reaching outward, helping us to perceive the world around us more fully.

It's like the difference between a human eye, with a single retina, and a fly's compound eye. Made up of thousands of different visual detectors, a fly's eye is exquisitely sensitive, enabling it to react far faster to changes in its environment. When a knowledge-mindful leader taps into their full network and leverages the knowledge and insights of their entire organization, they similarly gain a broader perspective, enabling them to react faster and make better decisions even amid the chaos of the VUCA world.

In finding this window to collective wisdom, the knowledge-mindful leader recognizes that they aren't simply pushing levers to order a machine to crank out more product. As such they recognize that what really matters isn't their own skills or experience or expertise—it's the way they can leverage their wisdom to cultivate wisdom in others, both individually and collectively. The wisest leader, after all, is the leader who knows how to lead *others* to wisdom—and to draw on the wisdom of others to constantly amplify and elevate the knowledge and wisdom flowing through their organization.

How to Start Building Bridges

It's in the window between the leader and their organization—between self and other—that this magic happens. You can't just chart the right path and issue a command. You need to connect with those around you and use those connections to create a culture of empowerment, engagement, and evolution.

Of course, our social relationships and capacity to communicate are fundamental to that process. This is always true: we are social creatures. As the poet John Donne put it, we are all "involved in mankind" and as much a part of everyone else's universe—"a piece of the continent, a part of the main"—as *their* individual world is a part of our own.[40]

According to the psychologist Nicholas Humphrey, in fact, it's our ability to see these connections and leverage our qualitative intelligence rather than our quantitative intelligence that truly defines us as humans.[41] In trying to manage and grow more mindful of our knowledge systems, our ability to envision and build

> *You can't just chart the right path and issue a command. You need to connect with those around you and use those connections to create a culture of empowerment, engagement, and evolution.*

bridges, and to understand and leverage social dynamics and ways of communicating, necessarily plays a vital role.

In a practical sense, connecting effectively with others requires an ability to see (and seek out) similarities instead of differences. Diversity, for the knowledge-mindful leader, isn't just a slogan or an abstraction—it's a critical reality, because it's through diverse perspectives and alternate ways of viewing the world that we unlock the full richness inherent in our systems of knowledge.

It's here that the knowledge-mindful leader's ability to anchor their relationships in their whole selves, and to deepen their engagement with others by drawing on their own spiritual dimension, becomes valuable, because our deepest values are generally *universal* human values. When you approach others with kindness, compassion, humility, and humanity, it becomes far more possible to connect with them effectively and on a much deeper level.

To build bridges to others, in other words, we need to build bridges between our own rich multidimensional selves—the full *totality* of ourselves, from the smallest parts of our ego and emotions to our rational mind to our spiritual dimension—and the world around us. That can feel scary: we're talking, after all, about allowing ourselves to be vulnerable and honest with those around us and to bring the things that matter most to us into direct contact with an uncertain and dangerous environment.

But that kind of engagement, drawing on our deepest traits and qualities and bringing them into connection with the world, is really what it means to reject the instinctual withdrawal and spiraling insularity that so many of us experience in the VUCA world. It's ultimately by drawing on the things that are strongest within us—our spiritual values, our emotional control, our human sense of identity—as part of a clear holistic sense of our full selves that we're able to strengthen relationships, engage forthrightly and confidently with others, and cultivate environments that provide a sense of belonging, growth, and high-bandwidth knowledge sharing for ourselves and everyone around us.

When you put this all together, it becomes possible to draw on your inner values and truths to guide your interactions with both situations and people in the outside world—and to integrate the knowledge gained thereby into your own deeper knowledge processes, validating and refining the mental models you use and cross-referencing them against your deepest values to ensure you stay on track even amid the chaos of the VUCA world.

That's a powerful approach for individuals, but also for businesses. Consider, for instance, the Swedish company Stora. Founded sometime between AD 850 and AD 1080 at a copper mine in Sweden, Stora endured ups and downs—including the Black Death!—but survived and thrived over the centuries that followed. It embraced new technologies, using water-powered pumps and unified management methods to drive new efficiencies and make Sweden the dominant force in Europe's copper industry. It branched out into forestry management and by the 1800s was producing silver, sulfuric acid, newsprint, and paint in addition to copper. In 1998 Stora merged with a rival papermaker to create the pulp and forestry giant Stora Enso—a remarkable new chapter for a millennium-old company.

Now, Stora didn't succeed just because it was lucky or wildly innovative or even unusually well managed. It succeeded—and survived the Reformation, the Industrial Revolution, and two World Wars—because its leaders got one thing right: they continually shifted their business model in response to the world around them. Over the centuries Stora has been a copper mining operation, a hydropower leader, a chemicals manufacturer, an iron smelter, and much more.

But Stora's bosses changed their business model by leaning into both their sense of the changing world around them and their deep convictions about what their company was. Stora didn't branch out into unconnected industries: it built on what it already was, deep down, and brought that into conversation with the changing world to unlock new opportunities and solutions to apparently intractable problems. "Stora ... managed to effect its dramatic changes without sacrificing its corporate identity or corporate life in the process," notes Arie de Geus.[42]

We can't simply imprint our goals on the world, of course. Part of our role, as leaders, is to understand the structures of the ecosystem in which we operate, to see how they place constraints on what is possible, and to find ways to either adapt to those constraints or work around them or—if possible—to change them and eliminate them.

But to find a road through these structural constraints, we also need to have a clear sense of what our organization is all about and where it should be heading. De Geus argues that companies like Stora succeed by drawing on a "memory of the future"—a vividly anticipated vision of the future that enables leaders to rapidly and effectively sort through and assign relevance to incoming information and leverage salient changes or facts to help them reach toward the future they've reified. The memory of the future is here akin to the deep-seated values that bubble up to guide our individual systems of knowing; they comprise a moral and intellectual and creative North Star that serves to guide us through the VUCA world.

Knowledge-Mindful Leadership

If you want to understand the power of knowledge-mindful leadership to effect change in your organization, think back on the attack on the Mumbai Taj in 2008, when heavily armed terrorists stormed the Indian luxury hotel. The violence was horrific, and dozens of people died. But the thousands of guests who escaped the hotel were struck by one thing: the incredible bravery and sacrifice of the hotel staff.

From the waiters who formed a human wall around guests to protect them to the banquet team who quickly helped guests to find shelter then spent hours handing out water and comforting them until they were finally able to evacuate, the Taj team came together to keep guests safe, support one another, and find creative solutions to the awful and unanticipated situation in which they found themselves.

What made the Taj employees so effective in a moment of crisis and so loyal to their employer that they were willing—in some tragic cases—to lay their lives down to protect guests? It was the leadership they experienced from their supervisors and managers each and every day.

The Taj Group has long been known for considering employees' values as well as their skills and qualifications when hiring new recruits. It is also known for training employees to be customer advocates and to draw on their core values to help them think on their feet during unexpected situations. Perhaps most importantly the Taj Group trains its *leaders*—from supervisors to senior executives—to constantly reach out to and check in with their direct reports, offering recognition and emotional support and actively soliciting employee perspectives on opportunities and challenges as they arise.

That's a sign of Knowledge Mindfulness in action at the organizational level, and it pays dividends. When employees are thrust into a moment of crisis, they know how to analyze the situation and how to respond quickly by drawing on their own whole selves to support both guests and colleagues. They are also *motivated* to find solutions, because they've been integrated into a culture that truly values them as people and trained by leaders who draw on their full multidimensional selves to engage, encourage, and support them.

Now, hopefully as leaders we'll never be called on to steer our organization through anything as awful as the Taj terror attack. But while the stakes may not be life or death, in a VUCA world, our organizations are constantly being thrown into unanticipated and deeply challenging situations.

The only way to prepare for and overcome those challenges is to lead with our whole selves—to draw on the totality of ourselves and engage mindfully with our employees in order to build cultures that bring out the best in them and empower them to rise up, reach out, and succeed even in the worst of times.

Through Knowledge Mindfulness, we can tap into our own best traits—our compassion, our emotional energy, our instincts, our rational minds, our spirituality—and use that holistic toolkit to reach out to others.

When we understand the full breadth and depth of our own systems of knowing—and thus our entire selves—we are far better equipped to forge strong and deep connections with others. It's by leaning into those connections that we are ultimately able to build systems and cultures within our organizations to nurture our employees, give them a sense of belonging, and communicate a powerful vision that can serve as the glue to pull diverse teams together into a cohesive and resilient whole.

Your awareness of and ability to shape your understanding of yourself and the world around you determine how well and how effectively you can shape the world around you and how well and how effectively you can lead, inspire, and cultivate others.

By intentionally building such connections, we reveal Knowledge Mindfulness to be much more than mere navel gazing: it becomes the guiding force that drives us all to see ourselves as part of a connected system and to leverage those connections to elevate both ourselves *and* the systems of which we're part. Knowing ourselves means recognizing that we are social beings, part of a larger global ecosystem—the self-regulating system that futurist James Lovelock calls "Gaia"—that binds us inextricably to all other living beings.

Recognizing this deep and universal connectedness—a connectedness that doesn't diminish our individual values and insights, but instead is strengthened and enriched by them—is the key to finding joy and meaning in a VUCA world. Verna Allee asks, "How would we describe the world of business if we told the story from the edges, instead of from the center?"[43] In much the same way, I would suggest, Knowledge Mindfulness helps us to look beyond and outside the narrow and insular stories we have, for too long, told about ourselves and the businesses we run.

In the VUCA world, we need knowledge-mindful leaders who are able to understand themselves. But we also need leaders capable of using that understanding to engage with and shape the world around them—and to thereby create caring, nurturing, and compassionate cultures through which knowledge flows smoothly and where social capital is abundant for everyone.

This requires confidence and clarity and conviction. But it also requires humbleness and an ability to accept the constraints of the VUCA world and the need to draw on and trust others in order to find a path to success.

This might seem like a paradox or a contradiction—but it's one that's easily resolved when you remember that Knowledge Mindfulness rejects reductive "either/or" dichotomies and asks us to understand the world through a "both/and" lens. In order to move confidently through the VUCA world, we need to allow uncertainty to temper our actions and accept the limits of our personal knowledge so that we can reach out to and make the most of the knowledge that *others* bring to the table. Confidence and humility are both powerful tools, and it's by using them *both* appropriately depending on the circumstances that the knowledge-mindful leader turns other people's knowledge into a potent resource that they can leverage across their own systems of knowing.

When we approach using only our emotions, or only our rational mind, we may be able to forge a connection—but the connection will often be fleeting or brittle. It's by bringing our *whole* selves into play, and leveraging *all* our systems of knowing, that we become able to forge deeper and more durable connections with individuals and to build trust, loyalty, and a deep-rooted culture of knowledge sharing across our organizations.

Confidence and humility are both powerful tools, and it's by using them both appropriately that the knowledge-mindful leader turns other people's knowledge into a potent resource.

This holistic, connected insight enables knowledge-mindful leaders to see that other people's viewpoints represent valuable alternate perspectives on the challenges they are tackling. Knowledge, they realize, is itself an emergent phenomenon: it is a universal experience that unites us all, yet every individual's experience is unique to them. This might initially sound solipsistic, but in fact it's the opposite—because it's in the aggregation and interaction of all these unique experiences that new patterns, new possibilities, and new ways of knowing (which I term "collective wisdom") come to fruition.

The VUCA world might seem overwhelming and impossible for any individual to navigate effectively. But Knowledge Mindfulness is grounded in the insight that we can *cocreate* our reality: we don't *have* to navigate the VUCA world alone. It's by embracing that fact and drawing on our understanding of ourselves to connect with others and cultivate connections across our organizations that we can build dynamic organizations that are optimized not just for efficiency, but for the flow of knowledge.

In this way, Knowledge Mindfulness offers a remedy for the alienating cycle of ignorance that plagues us as individuals. But it also offers an alternative to the destructive and limiting logic of Taylorism. It's by cultivating deep and effective connections—between human individuals, within our own organizations, across other organizations, and beyond—that we can capture the emergent properties of knowledge, move beyond being merely mechanistic *managers*, and evolve into the *knowledge-mindful leaders* our organizations need to thrive in a VUCA world.

Part 3:

Zooming Out:
The Moving Engine of
Knowledge Mindfulness

Chapter 5

The Path to Knowledge Maturity

I've already shared with you the way that the first day of COVID lockdowns affected me—how I wandered the streets of Boston trying to figure out what to do next and how that led me, little by little, to reevaluate my path, change my career, forge new connections and new understandings, and eventually come to write this book.

For me the turmoil was a trigger. It forced me to ask tough questions about where I was and what I wanted and to think through what my real purpose was in life. It was, in fact, the moment when I stopped thinking narrowly about knowledge management—the field of study I'd dedicated myself to for years!—and started thinking instead about how to elevate and evolve my own understanding and use of knowledge in my own life.

I stopped asking simply how to use knowledge and started asking questions about what knowledge was and how it could be better managed. I started questioning my own knowledge, second-guessing things I'd taken for granted, and looking for new possibilities.

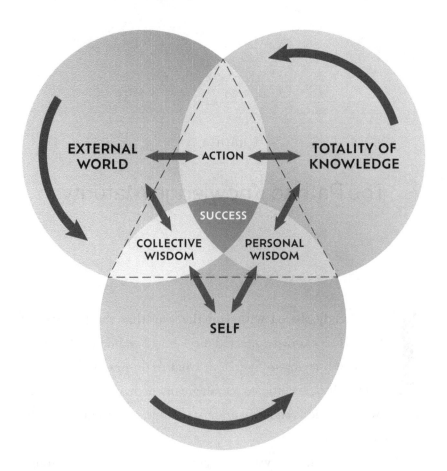

That led me to develop the framework I now describe as Knowledge Mindfulness. But the more I dug into these topics, the more I realized that I wasn't just mapping out a new theory. I was changing something profound about my own perspective on knowledge and its role in shaping my life. The more I applied my new learnings and under-standings in my own life, the more I found that I was able to act with clarity and conviction—to create, to expand my understanding, and to succeed—and to bring others along for the ride too.

My work on Knowledge Mindfulness, in other words, was both driven by and itself driving a fundamental shift in my own mindset.

I was questioning, reassessing, and exploring in ways I hadn't done for a long time. In exploring Knowledge Mindfulness, even without knowing it, I was going on a personal journey toward what I now call **personal knowledge maturity**.

As we move into these final chapters, I'd like you to start by thinking back on the "three circles" we previously discussed: the totality of our knowledge, our self, and the external world.

We've seen how these three areas each play key roles in shaping the systems of knowledge of which we're part. And we've seen, too, how the intersections between those areas are really windows of opportunity—windows in which we have space to work on elevating our knowledge maturity to achieve personal wisdom and collective wisdom and to have a positive impact on the external world through our actions.

Now I want to ask you to remember that those three windows aren't *isolated*—they're deeply connected! In fact they form what I call the **golden triangle** of Knowledge Mindfulness—because when they work together in harmony, they become the engine for long-term sustainable transformation and growth for yourself, others, and your entire organization. Personal wisdom sparks collective wisdom, which drives smart actions, which accelerates your journey toward personal wisdom, and around and around we go—a constant cycle of self-improvement, engagement, and elevation as you continue your journey toward knowledge maturity and bring others along for the ride.

> *Personal wisdom sparks collective wisdom, which drives smart actions, which accelerates your journey toward personal wisdom—a constant cycle of self-improvement, engagement, and elevation.*

Harnessing the Three Cs Loop

So how can you make the connection between the ideas we've already spoken about—some of them theoretical or even esoteric—and the practical reality of living and leading in the VUCA world? In the chapters that follow, I'll explain just that by asking you to think about elevating your knowledge maturity in terms of enhancing the knowledge flow—the engine that will help to transform our business and our life by building and enhancing our three core *supercompetencies*.

What's a supercompetency? Well, as leaders, we have many different competencies, from our ability to communicate our vision to investors, to our ability to inspire a team, to our ability to keep our company's finances in order. Our ability as leaders can be thought of as the sum of these competencies—our ability to formulate and articulate a vision, assess and adapt to the circumstances we find ourselves in, make smart decisions, influence others, and make our organizations the best they can be.

What I'm going to be talking about, however, are the metacompetencies that enable us to enhance and improve these other more day-to-day competencies. That's why I refer to them as *supercompetencies*—they're the superpowers that let you do everything *else* more intelligently and effectively. When we enhance these metaskills, we're able to enhance our other competencies (from information literacy to communication to creativity and beyond) and to operate more effectively across many different capabilities, effectively hitting many birds with a single stone.

It's by learning to deploy these supercompetencies—collectively, not in isolation—that you can transform all you've learned about Knowledge Mindfulness into a cohesive and actionable strategy for driving you, your team, and your organization to a higher and more holistic level of success. This is why I call it an engine: it's where we generate the power to transform and elevate both ourselves as individuals and the organizations we lead.

So, what are these amazing superpowers? Together, I call them the Three Cs Loop, because as we'll see, they're interconnected and feed back into one another, driving transformation by facilitating the flow of knowledge between self and the external world. Take a look:

1. Create (yet keep renewing)

Every leader needs to use knowledge as a creative and transformative force—and to keep driving that creativity back in on itself, to refresh and renew the generative processes and methods of learning that power us forward.

If Picasso had gotten stuck in his Blue Period, after all, he'd be remembered as a minor artist. It was his commitment to using everything he'd learned to find *new* ways of acting and creating, and then to harness *those* insights to learn in entirely new ways—to unlearn and renew his knowledge—that made him such a success.

Like Picasso we need to keep on challenging and reinventing ourselves by continuously regenerating and renewing our knowledge systems and to empower our teams to do the same in order to find new ways of succeeding—and new ways of thinking about success.

2. Connect (yet keep disconnecting)

For leaders, our knowledge—and our knowledge maturity—isn't much good if we keep it to ourselves. We need to be outward facing and engaged and work intentionally to connect with those around us.

That means being and behaving in an open, inclusive, respectful, and trustworthy way and connecting from a deeper and more integrated sense of self anchored in a "we" rather than an "I" identity. It also means creating a nurturing climate where others can flourish and share more than mere information but also bring their more authentic selves into the conversation. Above all it means finding ways to make our knowledge maturity resonate across our entire ecosystem: we need to elevate the knowledge maturity of those around us and learn to drive results that benefit *everyone*—from our employees and investors to the broader environment of which we're part.

Paradoxically, though, the path to knowledge maturity also requires us to disconnect. It's by tuning the world out that we can best connect with the totality of ourselves and avoid getting caught up in the noise and momentum of the world around us. Knowledge maturity thus requires a "both/and" approach rather than an "either/or" approach. We must constantly turn out toward the world *and* turn inward, toward the totality of our own knowledge and selves, in order to truly drive enduring success.

3. Capitalize (yet keep acting)

A knowledge-mindful leader understands that knowledge isn't simply something to amass and refine—it's something to build, share, and use continuously. Knowledge is a fast-moving river, not a pond full of stagnant water. The real test of knowledge maturity is your ability and willingness to keep that river flowing, open, and refreshed—not just for your benefit, but for the benefit of everyone around you.

The key, however, is to remember that successfully capitalizing on your knowledge to achieve your goals in any given moment isn't necessarily a sign of knowledge maturity. Knowledge maturity can certainly help with shorter-term and concretely tangible goals, but it also depends on recognizing the importance of long-term goals and intangible results.

We need to orient our actions around holistic goals—from helping ourselves to helping others and encompassing both tangible results (such as money or innovation) and intangible results (such as fulfilment and personal growth). The key is to draw on your insights about knowledge to make your action more intelligent and effective—and thereby generate better results for you and those around you.

Knowledge maturity, then, requires us to capitalize on our knowledge to achieve success—but not to see our successes as an end point. Even when things go right, we should keep on experimenting, testing, and acting on our knowledge and seeking new opportunities and potential connections that can carry us further onward and upward.

Knowledge maturity, in other words, reflects your capacity to integrate the principles of Knowledge Mindfulness into your own life, expanding and transcending the totality of your knowledge. It can be thought of as the degree to which you use the processes and tactics of the Three Cs Loop to integrate the principles of Knowledge Mindfulness into your life and work.

The Rules of the Road

We'll discuss each of these supercompetencies in much more detail in the chapters that follow, and I'll list plenty of tactics you can take to evolve your capabilities in these key areas.

Before we embark on that journey, though, I'd like to ask you to keep in mind a few simple overarching rules or guidelines. They aren't complicated or difficult, but they frame everything else we'll be working on. If you can keep these guidelines in mind, then everything else will fall into place.

1. **Keep questioning your knowledge.** Knowledge maturity starts with three simple questions: *what* do you know, *why* do you want to know it, and *how* can you use the Three Cs Loop to close the knowledge gap? If you're ever at a loss for how to apply Knowledge Mindfulness in your life, try asking yourself these questions—about a situation, about a person you're dealing with, or (especially) about yourself and your own knowledge.

2. **Keep striving for objectivity.** In asking these questions, it's important to be as realistic and objective as possible. We all naturally see the world through a subjective lens and tend to overstate or understate our responses to personal or probing questions. There's no judgment here, but to drive results you need to keep pushing for honest answers, even if it means delving into uncomfortable territory.

3. **Keep pushing for a deeper understanding.** As you ask and answer these questions, remember the purpose behind them. Are you trying to solve a short-term problem or untangle a big systemic issue? Are you tugging at one thread when you should be dealing with another? The more you ask these questions, the more you'll see the connections that link small problems and big issues or yourself and others.

4. **Keep thinking holistically.** This kind of connected thinking is critical as you draw on the Three Cs Loop, because these supercompetencies are themselves part of a bigger system of

knowledge maturity. It's when things work together that the magic happens! So don't think of any one part of this process in isolation—keep working to see not only how creativity, connectedness, and capitalizing on our knowledge operate, but also how renewal, disconnection, and continuous action work together as important forces driving you forward on your personal journey to knowledge maturity.

5. **Keep moving forward.** Above all else remember that knowledge maturity is a continuous journey onward and upward. Stagnation is the enemy: if you feel like you're getting too comfortable, try shaking things up! You need to work to ensure you never lose a sense of excitement and enthusiasm for the feeling of "not knowing"—because that uncertainty and hunger to know more is what keeps us alive and kicking forward. The goal is to constantly work to evolve and elevate your understanding and seek new ways to connect and expand your usage of the Three Cs Loop to raise your performance as a leader and also your fulfillment and vivacity as a human being.

These guidelines are a reminder that the journey to (or toward) knowledge maturity depends on a kind of creative tension. You need to understand, but *also* dwell in a place of inquiry and questioning. You need to zoom in on and utilize the granular details of your knowledge, but *also* zoom out to see the bigger picture and the larger system of which you're part. You need to fight against ignorance and constantly onboard and retain new knowledge, but *also* keep an open mind and be willing to subvert or challenge all the things you think you know.

That tension also manifests in the push-pull relationship between realism and visionary imagination. It's no good wishing things were other than they are—you need to work with what you've got! But you also need to anchor that realism in a higher purpose: the knowledge-mindful leader doesn't try to fight the tide, but they are still capable of dreaming big, setting out visionary goals, and proactively modifying and evolving both their goals and their actions to drive purposeful and effective results.

Unifying these opposing forces, and living in and leveraging the tension that results, is the real meaning and promise of not only developing a holistic understanding of knowledge, but also reaping its benefits. It's a bit like the way an atom is constantly being pushed apart by electromagnetic forces but held together by the nuclear strong force—or the way the universe itself is being held together by gravity but also driven apart by the power of dark energy. Through Knowledge Mindfulness, you can see the totality of which the opposing forces are part—and, instead of being torn apart, use that tension to drive you forward.

In other words we need to leverage holistic understanding and awareness to balance the different forces across our own knowledge systems—the push and the pull, the yin and the yang—to keep expanding and elevating our own knowledge maturity across the entirety of our journey through this world.

The key, in all of this, is intentionality: you need to *commit* to continuously elevating your personal knowledge maturity. You will need to continuously strive to

> You will need to continuously strive to master the tension between knowing and action and to use Knowledge Mindfulness to create excitement and enthusiasm.

master the tension between knowing and action and to use Knowledge Mindfulness to create excitement and enthusiasm as you explore and engage with the world around you.

They say every journey starts with a single step. So, let's take our own first step forward—and start looking at the ways that we can use specific practices to hone our supercompetencies and elevate our knowledge maturity.

Chapter 6

Create (yet Keep Renewing)

W e're trained from early childhood to think of learning as being a simple, mechanistic process of onboarding knowledge from the outside world, a bit like a fireman shoveling coal into the furnace of a steam locomotive.

This is, however, a very linear and prescriptive way of thinking about learning and about knowledge itself. I hope by now you've come to see that knowledge and learning are far richer and more complex than can be captured by a process of merely consuming something from outside.

What we bring in from the outside world does matter a great deal, of course. But we also need to think about the knowledge we bring up from within ourselves and the knowledge we gain about the processes that shape our interactions both with the world outside and with our own inner knowledge processes.

Learning, in other words, isn't static or linear. It's interconnected and in constant motion: not a line but a cycle of exploration, self-discovery, and creative reintegration. I always think, in this context, of James Joyce's *Ulysses*, in which the protagonist, Leopold Bloom, remarks to himself, "Think you're escaping and run into yourself. Longest way round is the shortest way home."[44] That sense of perpetual returning—of journeying ever outward and seeing yourself reflected in each new horizon—is at the heart of Knowledge Mindfulness too.

I've spoken repeatedly about Knowledge Mindfulness as a journey, and it is—but the more you travel, the more you'll realize that the journey isn't from A to B. It's from A to B, and then from B to A, and then from A to B again! This isn't a linear journey: it's a cyclical process and a constant interaction between the knowledge you have about yourself; the knowledge you have about the world around you; and the decisions you make, the actions you take, and the impact you have as a result.

Creativity and Knowledge Generation

Importantly, though, the looping, circular nature of this journey isn't entirely repetitive—it doesn't lead to stagnation. Closing these loops, and continuously iterating and making connections, is how transformation takes place: it's the best way to elevate our knowledge maturity and unlock new ways of seeing, hearing, thinking, and acting in the world.

Think about the solar system: seen from one frame of reference, it looks like the planets are tracing circles around the sun. But the deeper reality is that the entire system is whizzing through space at 140 miles per second, so those circular or elliptical orbits are actually corkscrewing pathways through space—anchored around the sun, but also always in perpetual forward motion. It's the same in our knowledge systems: as we move beyond linear thinking and toward systems thinking, we'll keep closing the loop, and that in itself will become the impetus that keeps us moving forward.

Part of what drives that forward motion, of course, is our ability to mindfully *create* and *generate* new knowledge and to keep renewing it—to unlock our creativity, to learn in new ways and for new purposes, to *un*learn things that no longer serve us, and to drive effective innovation across our organizations.

Crucially, Knowledge Mindfulness also helps us to identify *barriers* to learning—the roadblocks and hurdles (which variously operate at the level of the individual, the team, and the organization as a whole) that lead to individuals and teams missing opportunities, getting stuck in ruts, and failing to creatively acquire internal and external knowledge to unlock new *ways* of knowing.

As we move through the tactics you can use to mindfully accelerate and cultivate these processes of knowledge generation and integration, remember: creating knowledge is just one piece of the puzzle. It's an important piece, yes, but the magic only happens when it's leveraged as part of a connected whole.

Learning and Leadership

No matter how hard you try, in a VUCA world, you can't depend exclusively on the knowledge that comes from the external world—or exclusively on the knowledge that comes from within yourself. You need the totality of your knowledge, and that means using both in harmony, in an understanding of how they each interrelate—and shape your decisions, interactions with others, and impact in the world—in order to drive results.

You need to understand, too, that just as knowledge isn't linear, it isn't something that *only* exists inside you. It's something that you manifest and reify through your communication, behavior, and actions and through the ways you help others to learn and to leverage their knowledge in impactful and enriching ways.

Learning and leadership, in other words, go hand in hand: it takes a well-led and well-connected team to keep expanding your organization's horizons and drive your knowledge forward. By integrating new ways of learning—from the world, from within—you'll find yourself drawn to new ways of leading, too, and to new strategies for helping others to generate and renew their own knowledge resources.

> *By integrating new ways of learning—from the world, from within—you'll find yourself drawn to new ways of leading, too, and to new strategies for helping others to generate and renew their own knowledge resources.*

Now, let's look at some specific strategies and tactics you can use to accelerate this process in your own personal and professional life. Remember, these are only pointers: the strategies you'll need will change over time, with some becoming more relevant than others according to the specific situations you encounter.

1. Read different newspapers.

Writing in 1919, the American writer and muckraker Upton Sinclair declared, "I read several newspapers, in the hope of getting the truth from one of them."[45] Reading widely, and getting your information from as many sources as possible, is something I always encourage people to do—because, after all, no single newspaper (or any other source of information) can ever give you the whole story.

For knowledge-mindful leaders, a key part of our task is to make sure we're acquiring high-quality, reliable, credible, and diverse information from the outside world. That means actively working to expand our own horizons and to draw from a diversity of sources—not just newspapers, but media and websites, researchers and rivals, consultants and customers, friends and family, and so on and so forth.

Reading more newspapers is just the beginning: research shows that on social media, for instance, people naturally organize themselves into groups of like-minded people—and that quickly leads to the emergence of echo chambers in which fresh viewpoints are drowned out. As leaders we need to fight this tendency on both the individual and the organizational level to ensure we're constantly seeking fresh insights and validating our worldview against other ways of perceiving and thinking.

You need to actively pursue novelty and new and opposing perspectives, and actively work to open your ears and your mind and your heart to them, in order to ensure the steady flow of fresh ideas that you need to elevate your knowledge. The more open you are to new perspectives and the more you value them and seek them out, the richer your own insights will become and the more fluidly knowledge will flow through your organization as a whole.

2. Nourish yourself.

In today's modern world, we track all kinds of things about our bodies. I have an app on my phone that records what I eat—not just the calories, but the balance of micronutrients—and lets me know if

I should be eating more kale to drive up my calcium levels or ordering the chicken to boost my protein intake. I have a fitness tracker, too, that monitors my steps, my heart rate, my blood oxygenation, and even my sleep patterns.

We need to be similarly mindful of our knowledge biometrics too. That partly means keeping track of how you're operating: are you bringing your best energy to the challenges you face, and are you using your time effectively? But it also means considering the knowledge and information you're paying attention to and onboarding: are you getting a balanced diet of incoming information? Are you being mindful about what you put into your mind and taking in things that serve you well— or are you ingesting misinformation, fake news, and other toxins that will impede your performance and your whole being?

This is especially important because, if I eat some dodgy seafood, I'll soon feel my stomach grumbling about it. But if I start onboarding bad information, the signs are much subtler. I won't have a direct physical reaction—I may even find that I'm *happier* with my bad knowledge, at least in the short term, because it won't challenge or discomfit me. Over time, though, I'll find my knowledge systems begin to operate less effectively: I'll see the world less clearly, and my subjective impressions of the world will be filtered through a fog of misunderstanding (of myself *and* of the world around me). That, in turn, will show up in the decisions I make and the goals I set myself and in how happy (or unhappy!) I become along the way.

Onboard enough bad information, and you can even wind up in a situation in which your knowledge systems are so degraded that you don't *realize* they're operating poorly. So, pay close attention to tracking the information you onboard and use to generate knowledge. Cast a broad net, but be critical and thoughtful about the ways in which you integrate new information into your existing systems of knowledge.

3. Surface your full self.

Opening yourself to diverse sources of information while still staying mindful about how you onboard information requires a willingness to surface and interrogate *all* the dimensions of ourselves: our biases, our emotions and negative feelings, our ego, and our values. That can be uncomfortable, because we tend to tell ourselves a single story about who we are and what we want and to see ourselves as entirely rational and transparent. Recognizing that the truth is more complex and that we're impacted by previously unrecognized biases or emotions can be a difficult process!

The reality, of course, is that *everyone* has biases and other hidden motivators of one form or another, and we use them to judge and filter out information that we encounter. The point here isn't to strip away biases entirely. That's a fool's errand: we'll always have biases, and in fact we *need* some biases to help us act quickly and efficiently in a VUCA world. If someone lies to me repeatedly, I'll develop a bias against the information they offer me—and that isn't a bad thing! It's a useful heuristic, a rule of thumb that helps me to sort out incoming information and separate the wheat from the chaff.

The key is to use those biases consciously and mindfully. A bias that you are aware of and know how to compensate for when necessary can be a useful thing; an uninspected bias, or one you're entirely unaware of, will distort your view of the world and limit the information and the possibilities you're able to unlock.

This is where the interplay between the knowledge that rises from within and the knowledge that we focus on from the world outside becomes extremely important. You need to keep surfacing and testing your biases against the information you bring in from the outside world and also against the deep values you hold. In other words you need to elevate your knowledge of yourself in order to elevate your knowledge of the world, and vice versa!

4. Codify your insights.

Your sense of self can be a slippery thing! If you discover a bias but don't do anything to formalize that new understanding, you'll often find that your new understanding will slip through your fingers as your biases retreat back into the shadows—not gone, but unacknowledged once more.

The way to translate glimpses of understanding into enduring insights that can become powerful creative forces is to record and codify them. Keep asking questions, of course, but make sure you put just as much energy into setting out your answers in ways that you can memorialize and return to.

What does that look like? The classic approach is to keep a journal and to use writing as an opportunity for ongoing reflection on yourself and the world around you. Other approaches might include mentoring relationships with a trusted advisor, or therapy, or talking things through with your spouse, or art projects. There's no one answer here—the key is to put clear processes in place to bring your biases, emotions, and other hidden aspects out into the sunlight.

The less comfortable we feel acknowledging an aspect of ourselves, the easier it will be for any insights we achieve to slip away and become tacit or unacknowledged once more. Every knowledge-mindful leader needs to find their own system or process for fighting that tendency and holding on to the hard-won insights they surface about themselves.

5. Play devil's advocate.

For leaders our task is to help others to achieve a similar level of insight in their own lives—to ask the questions and provide the strategies that can help them to grow, create knowledge, and renew their own knowledge system. We do that through our interactions with them and also through the processes we put in place and the culture we build in our organizations.

One key strategy when helping others to "learn how to learn" is to start playing devil's advocate. Ask questions that cut against the assumptions people have or that force them to justify the goals they've set and the strategies they're using to achieve them.

The devil's advocate paradigm is useful in part because people recognize it as such. You aren't attacking them—you're explicitly engaging in a process of asking questions to test out new ways of thinking, surface biases or emotions, or try to unlock new insights. Just as people recognize the value in brainstorming, they recognize the value in asking difficult questions to validate and test ideas.

When you keep asking questions in this way, without putdowns or judgment, you create a safe environment for people to tell you what they really think, feel, and value. The more you achieve this, the more knowledge will flow freely through your organization.

6. Build future memory.

Digging deeper and challenging yourself (and others!) doesn't have to be purely reactive, conducted in response to the immediate situations and stimuli you encounter. In fact it's also extremely important to get ahead of the curve and anticipate *future* situations in which you could find yourself.

This is where the idea of "future memory" becomes extremely important. Once you've established your goals and your underlying purpose—that is, surfaced the core values that underpin the goals you've chosen—you can start to peer down the track and figure out what challenges and opportunities might arise as you move toward your goal. The more you do this, and the higher your knowledge maturity, the more impactful these goals will be for both you and the world around you, driving both tangible and intangible impacts.

These anticipated scenarios are called future memories for two reasons. First, they should be imagined until they are as vivid as a real memory. And second, through that process of internalization, they should enable us to recall them rapidly (as rapidly as an intuition, one might say) when we actually encounter a situation that resonates with the ones we've imagined.

You can't lay down future memories for every possible scenario that you might encounter, of course. But the more you anticipate possibilities, the less alien unexpected situations will feel to you. You'll feel more in control and less fearful and anxious. You (and your team) will be able to draw on a bigger tool kit and find the right approach more rapidly to help you creatively find an effective path through whatever challenges come your way.

As René Rohrbeck and Jan Oliver Schwarz note, laying down future memories isn't just about making people more focused on a specific goal. Sometimes, in fact, our process of building future memories may even lead us to *change* the goals we're striving toward! Building future memories empowers us to anticipate the different paths that might lead to our goal and gives us the confidence and clarity to adapt to novelty, draw new information into our knowledge systems, and innovate in integrated and goal-oriented ways. "The more memories of the future that are stored, the more receptive can an individual be to signals from the outside world," they write.[46] Very true, though I would add: the better the individual (and the organization) can use those signals to elevate and enrich their knowledge systems.

7. Create spaces for growth.

Besides bringing a questioning mind to your personal interactions with your team members, it's important to build formal structures and spaces that encourage growth. That can mean a variety of events: a show-and-tell event where teams or individuals can show off their latest breakthroughs or projects, for instance, or a workshopping seminar where people can bring problems they're struggling with and discuss them with people from other divisions in the organization in a bid to generate fresh strategies.

It can also mean specific experiences. Lots of organizations do annual off-site meetings in a bid to build camaraderie and energize their teams. That's fine as far as it goes, but why only do it once a year? It can be remarkably compelling to take field trips: perhaps your next planning meeting could be held at the local art museum or walking through a local nature preserve?

The key is to make these activities meaningful and enjoyable—not dull seminars that spoon-feed information, but dynamic and eye-opening events that encourage new ways of learning and invite change and creativity. Not every meeting can be run this way, of course, but breaking out of ruts and moving into new environments can be a great way to get the creative juices flowing and to jolt people into reconsidering entrenched biases and opening themselves to new ideas and diversified perspectives. A good sign is if your employees are being asked questions rather than simply given answers or if participants are thinking creatively in terms of what things *could* be rather than solely reflecting on how things currently are.

Breaking out of ruts and moving into new environments can be a great way to get the creative juices flowing and to jolt people into reconsidering entrenched biases.

Finally, it's worth considering how you can provide your team with access to entirely new perspectives and forms of knowledge. Are there online courses, or different online platforms, that could make new insights and ways of interacting more easily accessible or offer authoritative and powerful perspectives that could enrich your team's knowledge assets? Such resources are often very affordable, so look around for ways to bring new ideas and growth opportunities to your team.

8. Model what you're trying to teach.

The great physicist Richard Feynman was once asked to explain a particularly intricate problem in quantum mechanics to a roomful of undergraduates. He went away and considered the challenge, then came back and—showing admirable humility!—admitted it was beyond his abilities. "You know, I couldn't do it. I couldn't reduce it to the freshman level," he said. "That means we really don't understand it."[47]

Feynman's point was that the processes of teaching and learning go hand in hand: if you can't teach something, you might not know it as well as you think you do! And just as importantly, sometimes the process of teaching is, itself, a process of learning—because as you articulate or model an idea for others, you'll crystallize your own understanding of the material or principles you're covering and reveal to yourself new ways of considering the issues at hand.

That's a vital point, because as leaders we can only get so far by asking questions and talking to our employees. We also need to show humility and a willingness to recognize that our knowledge isn't set in stone, so that we can model the kind of growth and creativity we're trying to instill in our teams.

One key way to do this is by rolling up your sleeves and getting your hands dirty. If your team can see that you're actively working to try new things, to explore new options, and to experiment and play with possibilities, they'll feel they have permission to do the same. And if they see you seeking direct access to information sources and raw data and forming your own opinions, they'll feel energized and motivated to form their own interpretations and ideas, too, instead of simply taking in information filtered through the perspectives of others.

This is especially important when it comes to making mistakes. Of course, *repeated* mistakes shouldn't be accepted and may well be a sign that you're stuck in the mud and that no learning is taking place! But if your team sees you diving in and trying things out, and failing, and learning from that failure instead of self-flagellating over it, then they'll understand that isolated mistakes are opportunities and stepping stones to growth. They'll be more willing to cheerfully admit to mistakes and to open-mindedly discussing better approaches—and that will help the entire organization to thrive and find new paths forward.

9. Reflect and renew.

Part of the process of creating and renewing knowledge lies in recognizing that not every idea is a good idea. William Faulkner is reputed to have said that all writers need to learn to "murder their darlings"—by which he means strip away the florid turns of phrase to which they've grown attached until only the essential and truly important remains. Even the best writer, it turns out, needs an eraser on the end of their pencil.

Maintaining and elevating your knowledge system requires a similar willingness to break free from patterns of thought that no longer serve you and to find new and better solutions. For leaders the onus is on us to model this process for others, but also to proactively help people to find their own path to reflective renewal. Leadership, in this sense, is like shaping a living tree: branches need to be encouraged to grow in the right directions, and sometimes you'll have to be willing to prune a twig or even a branch so that the tree as a whole can flourish and grow to its full potential.

As leaders we need to create space—both physical and mental—in which we can reflect and renew. We need to work to recognize the barriers that limit those processes too. Often our own ego becomes our greatest enemy, leading us to think that we *already* know it all—and it's by making space for reflection that we break down that illusion and find the pathways that lead us to renewal and growth.

Modeling that kind of maturity is a great way to lead *others* to reflection and renewal too. You can't simply order your team to grow or dictate what they need to realize—because if you rob them of their process of reflection, they'll never find their own road to renewal. Instead of telling your team that they've failed or that their ideas are flawed, try encouraging them to reflect on how they arrived at a particular way of understanding a problem. Offer guidance instead of imposing control, and as the employees talk through and reflect on their own processes, they'll rethink things and start to question their own underlying assumptions.

The key is to ensure that your team knows that while the end results are important, what *really* matters is building the processes that let you replicate, refine, and elevate those results over time. That requires evolving your understanding, drawing on new sources of information, and constantly questioning and renewing your ways of thinking and acting—and making mistakes is a natural part of that process, as long as you acknowledge, analyze, and learn from them!

10. Stop trying to be right.

Many bosses think the best way to spur innovation and creativity is to argue with their employees—to browbeat them into trying new things and thinking harder about the problems they face. That often gets caught up in questions of ego: bosses want to look like the smartest person in the room, and they ask questions designed to promote themselves rather than to lift up others.

The knowledge-mindful leader understands that arguments are dead ends. What's really needed is engaged and elevating *dialogue* that goes beyond either/or constructions and actively seeks out new ways of thinking about a given challenge. Think about the art of conversation: a good exchange is precisely that—an *exchange*—with people taking turns to contribute, to listen compassionately (with our heart and soul, not just our ears!), and to build positively upon what the other person has to say. This is both an attitude and an attribute of our conversations: we need to bring an open mind, but also show people that we value them through the words we use, which have the power either to harm or to encourage others.

That holds true for even high-stake discussions, too: you should constantly be seeking ways to discuss topics that are constructive, not negative or destructive, and that lead to everyone feeling valued and heard. Sometimes, ironically, that means bringing more people into the room: it's easy for a two-way conversation to become oppositional or confrontational, but invite other people to give a third or fourth or fifth perspective and you'll often find new and more fruitful paths forward.

Be thoughtful about *who* you add to a conversation, too: creativity springs from the intersections between different disciplines, so it's often healthy to bring in a guest speaker from an area that might seem far removed from the business challenges you're facing. What would a biologist, an artist, or a network engineer have to say about your company's structure and strategy, for instance, and what might your team learn from looking at their current challenges through a completely different lens?

The key, of course, is to keep an open mind. If you win an argument, you've really lost, because you've reinforced your existing understanding rather than elevating it. The goal isn't to *be right*— it's to find the best possible way forward, wherever it comes from! Seek out new perspectives, and try to show that you take real joy in discovering that you're mistaken about something, and you'll find everyone in your organization will start to do the same. The best leaders are confident enough to show humility and to lower their defenses and admit mistakes if it leads to a better result for themselves and their team.

Keep on Creating

The key point in all of these methods is that knowledge creation and generation don't come simply from sitting in a classroom or reading a textbook and passively soaking up information. Knowledge Mindfulness tells us that learning is *always* active rather than passive, because what we ourselves bring to the process determines what we're able to take away from any given situation—and what we give back to the situation through our decisions and actions determines what *others* will learn too.

Knowledge, in other words, is a living system, in continuous motion, that manifests through our actions, our impacts, and our presence in the world. It's inherent in our behavior, in our connections to others, and in our ability to collaborate and to lead.

To create and renew our knowledge, we need to bring the totality of our knowledge to that process, drawing knowledge inward from outside and upward from within ourselves. Through creative and compassionate leadership, we need to help others to find their own way through the process, too, so they can mindfully and continuously generate and renew their knowledge in order to elevate their own knowledge maturity.

Chapter 7

Connect (yet Keep Disconnecting)

Talking to my son the other day, I was struck once again by how plugged in his generation is. Every few minutes his phone pinged with another update, another message, another shared link or tagged photo. "You must feel so connected the whole time," I said. "Well, yes," he said. "But my generation is *so* connected—all the time, to everyone—that we wind up feeling disconnected too."

That's the paradox of our fast-moving, high-tech, digitized, globalized world. We're constantly bombarded by information and messages and signals and content, but amid all the noise, it feels harder than ever to truly connect with other people. We wind up crashing into each other, pushing people away or jostling for space instead of recognizing all the things we have in common and the deep values we share.

Part of the reason for that is a kind of shortsightedness: we focus on the short term instead of also prioritizing the long term, on what feels urgent instead of what's truly important. Our sense of disconnection from *others* is symptomatic, in this sense, of our inability to disconnect from the hustle and bustle of everyday life, to connect inward—and then to use our whole selves (with all our knowledge, values, and intuitions) to more mindfully reengage with the world around us.

Without that process of disconnecting in order to reconnect, we wind up relating to other people (and the knowledge they reflect in their communication and behavior) in a very transactional way. We focus on words and facts, not wisdom and insight, and ask people to share their knowledge with us so that we can use it, right here and right now. Often, we've already decided what we're going to do with that incoming knowledge before we've even received it or tried to understand its content and context. We aren't open to being surprised or challenged by their knowledge, but simply see it as a resource to be exploited.

This kind of transactional connection is, by definition, pretty superficial. It skips over the possibility for deeper connections between human beings: even in the moments when we think we're connecting, in other words, we're often simply growing more isolated. This, of course, is exactly what my son was feeling: all those tweets and status updates and social-media alerts were no substitute for a real human connection.

A Better-Suited Way to Connect

Knowledge Mindfulness offers a path to a different way of connecting with self and others. The first step on that path is to recognize that connections aren't just a process of extracting knowledge from somebody else. They're *two-way* processes in which we share and exchange the totality of our knowledge with others and give and receive multi-layered feedback and support (in the form of knowledge, emotional support, social ties, and so forth) with the people we encounter.

Once you recognize that, it becomes clear that connecting with others depends not just on the knowledge you can gain from them in the short term, but on the relationships you can build over time. Instead of trying to maximize the amount of knowledge we can extract from someone in a single interaction, Knowledge Mindfulness asks us to focus on broadening the bidirectional knowledge-sharing bandwidth that defines our relationships.

To achieve this we need to move beyond intellectual "head-to-head" relationships and start building "head-and-heart-and-soul" relationships grounded not in fleeting and clinical transactions, but in meaningful long-term associations. When we connect this way, we're able not only to maximize our knowledge over time—but also able to inspire real loyalty and help those we lead to give their best willingly.

As should be clear, cultivating these kinds of connections requires us to draw on the totality of our knowledge, leveraging it holistically to elevate our knowledge maturity as we cycle through the many different elements of which it is comprised. Understanding both your constructed self and your deeper and more spiritual values lets you leverage both together in order to lead with integrity and honesty—and composure and presence in these turbulent times—to engender trust across your organization.

So how can you lead in ways that will create an environment where connectivity comes to the fore and where your organization will become a nurturing, creative, and loyal space for everyone? Let's take a look at a few key tactics.

1. Connect the dots.

To connect with others, we have to draw on the capabilities explored in the previous chapter to connect with our own selves and codify those learnings—then connect the dots by being open to connecting *with* our whole selves and to the *entirety* of the people we're encountering.

The goal here is to start bringing together our newly surfaced and codified insights and viewing them as themselves interconnected and part of a bigger system. It's by working to perceive the patterns that emerge from the things we reflect upon, and to identify or situate them in relationships with one another, that we're able to pinpoint the real issues that underlie the more superficial challenges we face.

To be clear: I'm not just telling you to dig deeper into any single challenge you're facing. Digging deep is important, but you also need to be able to step back and see the challenge as part of a bigger picture. It's by extracting deeper meaning and understanding that a clearer picture starts to emerge, and you arrive at truly actionable and powerful new ways of thinking about and solving challenges.

So, if you find yourself asking, "Why?" remember that you've only taken one step in your journey. If I dislike someone, I might ask, "Why?" and realize I'm having a bad reaction to some criticism they've offered me—but if I step back and start connecting the dots, I might then see that their criticism rubbed against some deeper insecurity that I feel and that the same insecurity is also to blame for the way I snapped at a worker who challenged me or for the perfectionism that makes it hard for me to complete a particular task on deadline.

It's seeing these patterns that let me drill down to address the *real* issues I'm facing and unlock solutions that solve not just a single specific challenge, but that drive systemic improvements across the entire network of challenges and opportunities with which I'm engaged. The key insight is that every question leads to more questions—and that it's by interrogating the *connections* between those questions and their answers that we can achieve a deeper understanding and start to find solutions that drive transformative and systemic success for ourselves and others.

2. Listen to others to find your blind spots.

As you forge better connections with others, you'll find that you're able to close the loop, using the insights they bring and the fresh perspectives they offer you to elevate your understanding of yourself and those around you.

This is vitally important because you never know what you don't know—so you need other people to help fill in these invisible gaps! Remember, the term "blind spot" doesn't just mean something you can't see. It refers to the area where the optic nerve meets the retina—a spot where your brain automatically "fills in" the gap to present a seamless view of the world. What's missing isn't just the missing piece—it's the awareness that there's something missing in the first place!

As we connect with others, we're gaining vital opportunities to identify and account for our own blind spots and to uncover missing pieces that we hadn't *realized* were missing in the first place. We're also bringing the same insights to others, of course, and participating in a mutual process of elevation as we collectively triangulate our way to a fuller and more accurate impression of ourselves, each other, and the situations we're in.

As leaders we need to be open to feedback and fresh perspectives and to raise awareness (in ourselves and others) of the fact that blind spots are structurally ubiquitous in both individuals and organizations. This is what makes connecting so urgent: we're simultaneously bringing our own perspectives to help others and drawing on their perspectives to elevate our own understanding.

Critically, we need to make sure that everyone understands that there's no shame in having blind spots and limitations. It's inherent to the experience of being human! We shouldn't be embarrassed by the things we don't know—we should relish the possibility of learning new things, participating in a bilateral (or, better yet, multilateral) process that helps everyone to see things in new and better ways.

3. Show that you care.

When you bring your whole self to the party and recognize the power of other people's perspectives, it becomes possible to recognize the individual struggles and challenges that those around you are facing as they work to align their own values and emotions with the problems they're facing and the work they're trying to do. Understanding these tensions makes it possible to guide people forward in ways that are simultaneously effective and compassionate.

> We shouldn't be embarrassed by the things we don't know—we should relish the possibility of learning new things, participating in a bilateral (or, better yet, multilateral) process that helps everyone to see things in new and better ways.

It's said that on the East Coast of America, people are kind but not nice, while on the West Coast, people are nice but not kind. That's vastly reductive, of course, but it's one of those jokes that has a big grain of truth at its center, because it speaks to the cultural values that dominate on different sides of the country. Our task as knowledge-mindful leaders is to try to fuse both elements in our leadership: we need to be kind *and* nice.

The niceness is in many ways the easiest part of the problem to solve, but it's often forgotten: as leaders we're under tremendous pressure, and it's easy to get grumpy about it. I always advise people to consciously work to start their morning with a smile and to make sure their first interaction with everyone on their team is pleasant and positive. Asking someone how their morning is going, how their kids are, or how their commute was helps to anchor relationships in the human, rather than in the specific problems and points of conflict that arise in business dealings.

We also need to make sure, though, that our niceness is anchored in real kindness—that we aren't just smiling, but that we're bringing real core values of love, care, and compassion to our leadership. When you smile at someone or share a small human interaction with them, use that moment not just to remind them that you care, but to remind yourself too.

Each pleasant interaction should be a conscious and intentional attempt to connect with your own spiritual dimension and to fore-ground your own personal ethical values. This isn't (or shouldn't be) just performative; if you connect with your whole self, and both surface and codify your values, you'll find your deeply held values will continue to emerge naturally and genuinely in ways that allow people to sense your authenticity.

4. Break down barriers.

Many biases are to do with in-groups and out-groups—the barriers that "naturally" emerge in any group or organization, whether it's between competing teams or groups of people of different ages or backgrounds. The knowledge-mindful leader understands that such perspectives are cultural learnings—a malleable part of our constructed self, not something set in stone. They understand, too, that while there are real differences between people, those differences can be reframed as an important asset, not a hindrance.

Age, for instance, is one of the most insidious barriers that we use to sort ourselves into these groups. When we're young we often look on those older than us as stodgy or conservative or boring, and as we age there's a tendency to start seeing those younger than us as naive, immature, or feckless. Knowledge Mindfulness leads to the realization that it's possible to build conduits that allow insights and perspectives to flow from one generation to another—in both directions!—so that the organization as a whole can leverage all the insights and knowledge assets at its disposal.

Again, this starts with building self-knowledge and then connecting the dots outward to the other: looking inward we might realize that we're dismissing a younger colleague's ideas, recognize that such behavior doesn't align with our values of openness and respect, then concretize our insight by putting a plan in place to actively seek their input in the future. At an organizational level, that might mean introducing mentoring without hierarchy: not just horizontal peer-to-peer mentoring, but mentoring that explicitly acknowledges that "too young to retire" employees can often benefit from the insights of younger or more junior employees, and that encourages a two-way exchange of knowledge and insights.

Similar approaches can be applied to break down cultural barriers and capture the value that diversity brings to organizations. At my husband's workplace, for instance, there's a giant video screen on the foyer wall that displays messages celebrating key holidays and other events for people of just about every possible faith or background. One week there'll be a message wishing everyone a Merry Christmas;

another week there might be messages in honor of Diwali or Eid. It's a small but highly visible gesture that simultaneously celebrates differences and underscores common values of shared respect, openness, and welcomingness.

A well-run organization uses visible displays of respect and creates rituals that affirm and foreground differences in positive ways to spark respectful conversations and exchanges of views. So don't try to flatten out differences—instead, revel in them, and seek ways to foreground our core human values, prime people to exchange knowledge and insights, and give them permission to bring their own values and cultural perspectives to bear on the situations they find themselves in.

5. Tell more stories.

Forging a unified organization without suppressing diversity can seem like a challenge. The key is to think of the organization as a macrocosmic version of the individual self. As we've seen, our individual selves are themselves multifaceted and multidimensional, and it's by recognizing that fact while *also* thinking holistically that we're able to achieve our potential. Similarly, the best organizations are diverse and multidimensional but are led with a holistic vision and sense of identity.

Building that sense of identity starts with turning inward and bringing your whole self—including your knowledge of who you are in terms of your identity, values, and priorities—to bear on the relationships you're trying to forge with others. But turning that sense of self into a sense of *common* identity also requires an ability to tell compelling stories that really build cohesion and a sense of shared purpose.

Think about a company like Apple, with its creation myth—Steve Jobs and Steve Wozniak, busy in their garage—and later its heroic rebirth under Steve Jobs's visionary leadership. Or think about the "HP Way," the egalitarian philosophy that helped make Hewlett-Packard great, which is really a story about the company's past, its leadership, and its continuing sense of itself.

Good stories don't just reflect a shared vision; they reflect and embody the values that a leader wants to enhance in their team and across their organization. Every fable ends with a moral, and many children's stories have moral lessons tied up in them—but because they communicate those lessons indirectly, they are much more powerful and effective, becoming part of the listener's emotional landscape. In the same way, leaders can use stories to touch people's hearts and souls—not just to tell them what matters, but to make them *feel* it, so they'll cherish those values and work to manifest them.

The best companies (and the best leaders) cherish these foundational stories and embed them into rituals and retellings that run through the company culture to give people a sense of real belonging. Stories become a framework that enables people from across the organization to overcome differences, connect, and work together to achieve common goals.

6. Provide opportunities for sharing.

Togetherness can arise from rituals, but there also need to be spaces where it can arise organically through chance interactions. Every office has a water cooler, a cafeteria, or some equivalent space where people gather to share bits of gossip, for instance, and often these places are powerful engines for knowledge sharing.

While such spaces usually arise accidentally, it's also possible to cultivate them mindfully, to create opportunities for serendipity to emerge and for conversations and connections to arise spontaneously. In Kuwaiti homes, for instance, we have spaces called *dewaniya*—a word that means a kind of sitting room, but also the informal meetings that take place in such a room. Through casual *dewaniya* gatherings, people come together to sip tea and put the world to rights, discussing the issues that matter to them—a participatory, collaborative, and frank exchange of views anchored in a shared sense of community.

Businesses can go beyond water-cooler chatter and create *dewaniya* spaces of their own. Perhaps every morning a different member of the executive team holds court in the cafeteria or in the foyer, chatting informally with anyone who stops by. Or perhaps you hold regular town-hall meetings that bring together representatives from different teams or departments—a place where people can share ideas, ask questions that might feel awkward in more formal meetings, and make their views known.

From after-work cocktails to weekend-long "hackathon" coding sessions, those rituals vary wildly from one company to the next—but at their core, they are always intended to bring the workforce together around a set of shared values and a shared understanding of what their organization is, what it stands for, and where they want to take it next. The key is to make sure there are safe spaces for discussion, where people can chatter freely—but where you can also mindfully encourage and shape interactions to ensure that people talk across, rather than just within, the groups and silos that naturally form in organizations.

7.   Make work more rewarding.

You can't simply order people to connect with one another or to give of their best in respectful and open-minded ways. Instead, you need to create environments that are simultaneously nurturing and demanding: places where people are expected to push themselves to do better, but where they are consistently recognized and rewarded and honored for the good they do.

This is an area where knowledge-mindful leaders excel, because they understand the value that rewarding connections brings for *both* sides. Nurturing someone else is really a way of nurturing yourself, and vice versa! This simple insight encourages them to challenge themselves to reach higher, but also to find ways to help others to grow and flourish, because they understand that it's only when we *all* achieve our potential that our connections can truly spark magic and the organization as a whole can really thrive.

This is important because it's something people don't always see clearly about themselves. We internalize the stories we tell about ourselves, and sometimes we need someone else—a leader!—to recognize that there are other stories that it's possible to tell. Consider someone like football star Lionel Messi: as a youngster he had plenty of talent but needed time to build up his self-belief. That's where a good leader was needed: even Messi needed the talent scouts to recognize the strength of his potential and bring him into a system of training and growth in order to build his self-belief and confidence to fully realize his nascent talent.

One example of the way that leaders can invest is by cultivating their team's potential. Starbucks, for instance, now offers all employees who've been with the company for three months or longer a fully paid tuition benefit that lets them get a bachelor's degree for free. Hewlett-

Packard has had a similar program for a long time, too, showing the importance of good leadership that invests in elevating the potential of your team. Such initiatives are an incredible way to show frontline employees that you see them as more than just a warm body—that you're hiring them for their minds, their knowledge, and their own whole selves, rather than simply to serve coffee or punch buttons on a cash register.

The more you, as an organization, go above and beyond for your employees, the more they'll do the same for you in return—and the more unified and connected to one another they'll feel too. The reality is that when you want others to give their best, you have to make them *want* to give their best. It isn't something you can simply take from them!

8. Hire for success.

Some of the best advice I ever got is that you should dress for the job you want, not the job you have. The same applies to organizations: you need to hire for the organization you *want* to be, because the people you hire today will determine what your organization becomes tomorrow.

This boils down to a question of identity, of course. When you know why your orga-

> When you want others to give their best, you have to make them want to give their best.

nization exists and what you want it to be, and when you understand and can articulate the core values that your company stands for, then it gets far easier to identify the people who share that organization's aspirations and vision of where it wants to go.

This is something you can concretize in your hiring processes. Just as Google famously asks people to solve algorithms or puzzles to get a handle on their analytical skills, so your organization can use narrative scenarios and role-playing to explore how people react to different situations and that reveal their values, beliefs, and ability to work with others. It can be as simple as walking people through the process of solving a complex problem: do they ask colleagues or seek help, or do they hunker down and try to solve it on their own?

Some of these desired traits can be addressed and reinforced during onboarding and training. Make your expectations clear and give people room to improve, and it's possible to coach people to connect: assigning an "onboarding buddy" or having new recruits shadow their bosses can be a great way to help people learn by observing and asking questions, for instance. But it's also important to recognize that some people simply aren't wired for the kind of organization you're trying to build. Sometimes, letting someone go is the best way to help everyone *else* to connect effectively.

9. Take time for yourself.

While connecting is vitally important, it's also important for knowledge-mindful leaders to model disconnection and to show their team the importance of taking rest and recovery time. Sometimes, it's when we're most engaged—immersed in a problem or pushing ourselves and our team to get something done—that we wind up slipping into learned patterns of behavior, rather than continually looking at challenges and opportunities with fresh eyes.

As I've described already, this sense of openness to new possibilities and new connections is something that the knowledge-mindful leader recognizes as incredibly important. To connect with others, you need to connect with yourself—and that requires giving yourself time and space to refresh your self-perception, resurface your values, and integrate your new learnings into your holistic sense of who you are. That's why I always tell business leaders that the best way to connect is to make space to *disconnect* and that the best way to lead a team effectively is to make time for themselves.

The goal is to disconnect not just by clearing your schedule, but by clearing your mind. Turn off your phone, and make time for rituals that help you to refocus: listen to birdsong or rain, take a long shower, gaze at the stars or the clouds, do deep-breathing exercises, take the stairs instead of the elevator. Do whatever helps you to find your way out of the noise and to a place of calm—spiritual, mental, and emotional—so that you can then mindfully reconnect with more focus and energy.

For leaders this is an area where modeling desired behavior is incredibly important. Take your vacation days, wrap up your workdays on time, and refrain from sending emails into the night. That way, your employees will understand that it's acceptable and desirable to disconnect and that doing so is a critical part of the process of building sustainable relationships and sustainable and effective knowledge systems.

10. Build a culture of connectedness.

When leaders take the time to know themselves and use that self-knowledge to help them know and connect with others, the entire team or organization they lead begins to grow into a healthier and more holistic sense of itself.

Individual workers will find their own paths to mindfully disconnecting and reconnecting, avoiding burnout and exhaustion and more playfully and joyfully reaching out to those around them. They'll take the time that's needed to assimilate new learnings and new knowledge into their broader knowledge system, and they'll return to the fray energized and able to think clearly about what *new* connections they need to work to forge.

Leaders can model this kind of behavior, but they can also cultivate it. Some leaders might insist on scheduling short breaks between meetings, say, or on arranging to hold a meeting in a park rather than a boardroom in order to help people break out of ruts and look at things with fresh eyes. Others might make a point of ensuring that employees take their holiday days—or, like Netflix, even offer employees an *unlimited* amount of vacation time so they can take full responsibility for when and how they connect and disconnect with their work.

Some organizations go further still: Google gives its workers one day a week to focus on projects of their own choosing, for instance, while 3M has accrued more than 22,800 patents thanks to a "15 percent time" policy that encourages workers to disconnect from their day-to-day work and chase new ideas.[48] Combined with a clear sense of mission and strong connections between individuals, such policies free people to look at challenges with fresh eyes, elevate their knowledge, and deliver incredible results.

Connect with Purpose

When you know how to connect with others and how and when to disconnect in order to connect in new and better ways, you'll find yourself acting with much more clarity and purpose in your life. Mindful connection is always anchored in a sense of mission, with a focus not only on the immediate task, but also on the deeper meaning behind it.

I saw a local news story the other day about a new construction project, and the reporter looked down into a trench to interview a workman laying an underground cable. "What are you doing right now?" he asked the man. Smiling, the guy looked up at him and said, "I'm building a refinery!" That's an incredible attitude: the workman was able to look beyond the trench he was crawling around in, or the cables he was sticking in the ground, and connect his work to the end result his organization was moving toward.

Our task, as leaders, is to ensure that everyone on our team understands not just what's expected of them, but why they're doing it and why it has so much value to the organization as a whole. Every small task is part of something bigger, and we need to communicate that clearly to our employees so they feel valued and so they feel their work has value. Making that connection encourages people to look outward rather than just keeping their heads down and focusing on their own small piece of the puzzle and creates new opportunities for connection and growth.

Remember, as a knowledge-mindful leader, you define the climate for your organization: you model the culture, because the work you do on yourself inspires the same kind of growth toward knowledge maturity in others. This is the power of Knowledge Mindfulness: it helps us to understand ourselves so that we can understand others and to connect with ourselves so that we can thereby connect with others—and bring their insights and knowledge back to augment our own self-understanding.

The more you come to understand yourself *and* others, and to connect with both, the more you'll find yourself living and leading with respect, compassion, and conviction. As you do so, those same traits and characteristics radiate out across your organization and make deeper and more profound human connections possible for everyone around you.

Chapter 8

Capitalize (yet Keep Acting)

Economists trying to get their head around our capitalist society sometimes use what's known as the yard sale model to show how money flows between people. The yard sale model asks us to imagine a group of people, each with the same amount of starting money—then has those individuals come together in pairs and gamble up to 20 percent of their total wealth on the flip of a coin.

That might sound fair and balanced, but inequities quickly emerge. Success and failure quickly become self-reinforcing: someone who loses money early on has less remaining to venture on future coin flips, while someone who starts off by winning will suffer less of a penalty if they lose on future rounds. Purely by chance the money in circulation accumulates in the hands of just a few players; keep going long enough, and virtually *everyone* will go broke, except for a single big winner.

Fortunately, the researchers studying the yard sale problem found a way to prevent that happening—by closing the loop and redistrib-

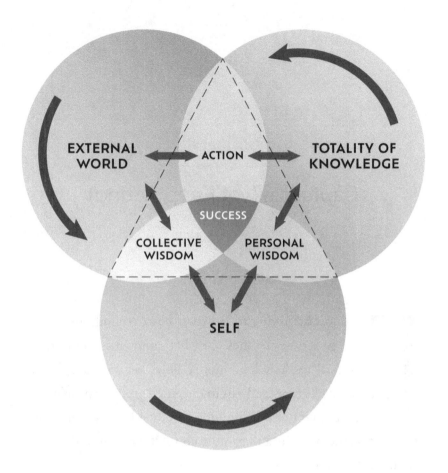

uting a fraction of each player's total wealth at the end of each turn. If players were "taxed" just 0.1 percent of their wealth and that cash was evenly divided among all the players, then what had seemed to be entrenched and unavoidable inequities quickly evaporated and the modeled society became far more stable and equal.[49]

Too many of us are still locked into a "yard sale" mindset when it comes to knowledge. We seek to maximize our own knowledge and hold it close, and to the extent that we think about others' knowledge, we focus on asking how we can put it to work to create value for us. The result, as with the yard sale problem, is that almost everyone winds up worse off: exhausted, isolated, and disconnected from the knowledge resources they need to truly succeed.

Knowledge Mindfulness tells us that it's possible to close the loop when it comes to our knowledge systems, much as researchers did with the yard sale problem. By being mindful of the health of the systems we're part of—by connecting with ourselves and with others, mindfully redistributing and sharing and reinvesting knowledge, deploying the totality of our knowledge, and bringing others along for the ride—it's possible to achieve far more, in far more equitable and sustainable ways, than we'd ever previously thought possible.

The Meaning of Success

To truly capitalize on our knowledge, we need to go back to the "golden triangle" of Knowledge Mindfulness—which, you'll remember, is really a way of talking about the smooth flow of knowledge that takes place when the Three Cs Loop is set in motion and works together as a single holistic engine for transformation and knowledge maturity. We've talked about how elevating our knowledge maturity requires us to operate across three key windows: the space for personal wisdom, the space for collective wisdom, and the space for action. As we move into this final chapter and think about how to truly maximize the value we get from our knowledge, I want to ask you to remember that there is no path to success that relies on *just one* of these windows.

Instead, success comes when we leverage *all three* windows in harmony. We can't achieve real success simply by elevating our knowledge to a new state of personal wisdom, or by elevating our collective wisdom, or by elevating our action. Success comes when we harness all three, turning them into a kind of flywheel that gains momentum as we use action to *spark* personal wisdom, and personal wisdom to *drive* collective wisdom, and collective wisdom to *spur* further action.

When we get these three things right—when we get them right *together* and use each part to elevate the whole—we can find our way to a new kind of success that isn't fixated simply on wealth or promotions or other tangible results. Instead, we can find a more *holistic* form of success that encompasses all of that but also the impact we have on others and the fulfillment we find in our own lives.

> *Success comes when we harness all three windows, turning them into a kind of flywheel that gains momentum as we use action to* spark *personal wisdom, and personal wisdom to* drive *collective wisdom, and collective wisdom to* spur *further action.*

This kind of success is the direct result of putting our knowledge into action. Knowledge Mindfulness is, perhaps above all else, a framework for taking the *right kinds* of action and making smarter decisions to solve real-world problems more effectively. But it is also grounded in the understanding that to get the best results, we need to materialize our knowledge in ways that reflect our increasing personal and collective wisdom—and keep on striving for *better* approaches, even when we've achieved remarkable degrees of success.

Success, in this way, can be seen as the ultimate result of knowledge maturity—though, of course, as we elevate our knowledge maturity, we'll realize that there's nothing "ultimate" about success. There's always more to strive for, and it will always be important to keep closing the loop and working to find new and better ways of turning our knowledge into effective action.

That is what we really mean when we talk about *capitalizing* on our knowledge. Working toward knowledge maturity doesn't just mean finding shortcuts to a particular kind of success or cheat codes that let you realize a certain kind of concrete value or tangible impact. It means understanding the interconnectedness of *all* aspects of knowledge maturity and leveraging them harmoniously and holistically to carry us—and the teams we lead—to new heights.

Let's take a look, now, at the ways in which leaders can harness this value-creation loop and drive success as they continue their own journey toward higher knowledge maturity.

1. Keep experimenting.

The most important thing to keep in mind when you're looking to level up your knowledge maturity to drive value is that there's *always* a better way of doing things. You're really in competition with yourself: if you've hit a roadblock where the old ways of doing things no longer work, it's up to you to figure out what that better way is and apply it across your organization!

That means staying hungry, staying open-minded, and staying curious—and using those attributes to drive playful experimentation across your organization. Experimentation means activating and training all our senses at once and "being" more fully. That means trying new things, of course, but also probing and testing old things—seeking to question the status quo, to seek out new possibilities, and to both validate and expand our existing understanding.

You need to have an explorer's mindset in order to test, refine, and verify or validate knowledge. Reconnect with your inner child, and relearn how to see things without the constraints that come with your constructed self! But remember, you also need to translate exploration into action: leverage the things you've found effective at a small scale to achieve quick victories, then amplify that success by encouraging other teams to apply the proven strategies you've developed.

Effective experimentation starts on a fairly small scale. The goal is to gather data and information, to verify and test it, and to feed it back into our understanding and our decision-making processes. It's a bit like when you design a product: you constantly test and prototype and iterate and validate. Well, your knowledge also needs to be constantly tested and iterated. It's like a living system: it keeps on changing and evolving, and you need to keep working to rethink, redesign, refresh, and revitalize your understanding.

By elevating our understanding in this way, we can make our perspective clearer, leading to a higher probability that our decisions will lead us to the success we seek. That won't necessarily be a direct path: sometimes, in refining your understanding, you'll uncover *new* problems or see difficulties that weren't previously apparent. That's fine too! The key, as knowledge-mindful leaders, is to demonstrate a willingness to experiment and the courage to act and take risks, so that your team will also gain the courage, trust, and self-belief required to drive innovation.

The road forward might not always be smooth, but we have to keep moving forward. A business that isn't adapting and growing won't survive. So keep experimenting, testing, and seeking new ideas and options.

2. Shake up the script.

Innovating doesn't just happen in laboratories or research hubs. Sparks fly every time two or more people come together and share ideas—if they're open to learning from one another and mutually building on those ideas. To enable that we need to ensure that we're able to embrace and lean into weird or surprising or off-script interactions and to see the value in them.

Recently, I went to the theater, and just as the star actress was delivering her closing monologue, a ringing noise came from somewhere in the audience. Someone had forgotten to silence their phone! The actress was startled out of the moment: you could see her face tense up, and she lost her rhythm. She had to close her eyes and recenter before she could continue with her scripted monologue, and the ending of the entire play was spoiled as a result.

In improv, on the other hand, participants are trained to embrace the unexpected. They are told never to say, "No"—instead, they have to say, "Yes, and …" If one actor walks on stage and says, "Have you seen my ostrich?" the other won't just say, "No," and keep doing what they're doing—they'll say something like, "Yes, and it just bit my grandmother!"—and by riffing on one another's ideas, a comic skit will quickly emerge.

To succeed as leaders, we need to learn to think less like scripted actors and more like improv comedians. It can be disconcerting to go off script—but it's by learning to navigate these unexpected moments and to capture the possibilities that emerge in small interactions and unanticipated ways of thinking that we're able to harness the full potential of all the different ideas and perspectives that ricochet around our organizations.

This doesn't mean reinventing the wheel every time we act. Once we've found a solution that works, it's okay to return to it! The key is to keep the basics in place while still leaving room to test new ideas: you might bake a cake according to a tried and tested recipe, but use different frosting or decorations, for instance. I use this approach when I'm giving lectures, too: the outline might stay the same, but I leave room to introduce new ideas, examples, or perspectives so that I can learn (or unlearn) and renew my ideas over time.

3. Manage change mindfully.

Turning new ideas into strategic change takes more than just an openness to serendipitous interactions, of course. Scaling new ways of doing things requires an ability to operationalize experimental concepts without overcommitting to unproven ideas—or scaring people off and losing their trust.

The best way to achieve that is to include your people in the change process, and secure their "buy-in." Start by recruiting a few influential team members to test and evaluate new ideas or strategies using small, manageable pilot projects. Ask them to qualitatively and quantitatively measure and validate the results—including the way people *feel* about the new way of operating. Reassess, fine tune, and see what works and what doesn't—and once you're 80 percent or 90 percent confident that you've found a viable solution, scale it up to a larger subset of your organization. Iterate that process until you're confident your new approach works, and you'll be able to scale with confidence—and to give your team confidence too.

Part of the key here is that by involving small groups in the pilot process, you'll turn them into advocates for the changes you're trying to enact. It won't just be you ordering change from the top—it'll be a process that other people feel ownership of and that they're invested in promoting to others.

The goal isn't just to make the business work better so that you get a promotion and investors get rich—it's to create benefits for everyone and promote values that everyone shares. The more you can deliver on that promise, the more people will see that and join you in your effort to drive things forward.

4. Humanize your knowledge markets.

Capitalizing on the knowledge flowing through your organization depends in part on ensuring that knowledge *does* flow through your organization and doesn't just gather dust in different siloed teams or departments. Every employee in your organization should be able to both contribute and receive tangible and intangible value, in ways that drive both their own success and the success of the organization as a whole.

Traditionally, organizations have sought to enable this by creating knowledge markets that allow people to discover, share, and trade data, solutions, and know-how of different kinds. This often looks a bit like a Yellow Pages or a Who's Who for the organization and helps people to identify topic experts that might be able to help them with a given problem. Often, though, such markets become sites of competition, too, leading people to vie to outperform one another rather than fostering collaboration.

As we elevate our knowledge maturity, we learn to temper our personal needs and promote mutually beneficial relationships for the sake of everyone. The knowledge-mindful leader seeks to introduce this kind of maturity to knowledge markets, too, creating exchanges that go beyond dry biographical or professional descriptors and humanizing the process of discovering and sharing data across the organization.

Instead of transactional exchanges—which, apart from anything else, require you to know in advance what you're trying to learn!—they promote more organic and direct connections between the members of their team. They create modes of exchange that are intertwined with emotions and values, not simply the transmission or extraction of information, and create opportunities for their team members to engage with their whole selves and the totality of their knowledge, even in the simplest conversations.

Trust plays a vital role here: it stands as the essential precondition for knowledge markets, since by their nature such markets are informal and not bound by enforceable contracts. Leaders need to encourage their employees to lean in and trust their counterparts and to recognize that every exchange that takes place across the knowledge market is (or should be) bilateral, with each side gaining something from the exchange. There aren't many altruists around these days: most people expect reciprocity in one form or another!

Spurring the development of more trusting knowledge markets can take many forms. Perhaps you might rotate key team members through different roles or business units or office locations, so they can forge connections with a broader cross section of the organization. Perhaps you might create forums, town-hall meetings, and mixers to provide opportunities for cross-functional conversations. Or you can create rituals that incentivize the free exchange of ideas, from pitch competitions to off-site brainstorming get-togethers.

Even a low-grade sense of crisis can help people to come together: overcoming challenges binds us together in a stronger way. To promote cooperation over competition, though, be sure to create a clear expectation of teamwork, to reward sharing, and to base performance appraisals on collective projects. It may also help to celebrate individuals' contributions to collective efforts by recognizing them in newsletters or ceremonies.

The goal is to go beyond simply cataloging technical expertise and to give people a chance to connect for the purpose of collaboration—enlarging the pie for everyone, or cooperating to create multiple pies, rather than fighting over who gets the biggest slice. Through meaningful conversations, participants will see new and bigger patterns emerge—and they will benefit from the full range of not just technical knowledge, but insights, perspectives, values, and everything else that makes up the totality of each individual's knowledge and thus the totality of the knowledge in your organization.

5. Don't let knowledge go to waste.

Humanized knowledge markets can help to expand the bandwidth of the knowledge exchange, but you still need to know what to do with the knowledge that's generated or discovered thereby. This requires a bias toward mindful affirmation—remember, try to say, "Yes, and ..." when you encounter a new idea!—and also a bias toward action. You don't need to accept every new idea uncritically, but you shouldn't dismiss it reflexively either.

A great example of this comes from Frito-Lay, where a junior custodian from a Hispanic background realized that the spicy chili powder his family sprinkled on their corn tasted delicious if you sprinkled it on Cheetos too. He called the company's CEO and pitched the idea—and instead of hanging up, the CEO really listened and saw the potential in the concept. The rest is history: Flamin' Hot

Cheetos are America's most popular snack and helped turn Cheetos into a $4 billion brand.[50]

There are plenty of examples of leaders who *don't* pay attention to the knowledge circulating in their organization too. In 1986 rocket engineer Roger Boisjoly told anyone who'd listen that NASA's space shuttle had a design flaw that meant it wasn't safe to launch in sub-freezing temperatures. But his deep understanding of the mechanics of the spacecraft's rocket engine wasn't acknowledged or acted on by senior leaders, so the Challenger launched as planned—and tragically exploded soon after takeoff.[51]

To seize opportunities and prevent catastrophes, knowledge-mindful leaders understand the need to listen openly to ideas—no matter where they emerge from—and to foster larger and more collaborative conversations to maximize the knowledge available in their organization to help them make smarter decisions. There's really no greater leadership sin than letting knowledge go to waste—so make sure you're open to new insights and that you're actively soliciting new perspectives and forms of knowledge from everyone on your team and building toward a meaningful consensus about what knowledge to leverage or scale up.

6. Share your authority.

Committing to not letting knowledge go to waste requires more than just a determination to be receptive to the knowledge you encounter. It also requires a willingness to trust your team and to empower the people around you to take action on their own authority in order to seize opportunities and turn knowledge into action.

One company that's great at doing this is Netflix: they're known for devolving authority from senior leaders out across the organization, so individual teams can take charge and put plans into action without waiting to be told what to do or given permission to act. "Sometimes I can go a whole quarter without making any decisions," says founder Reed Hastings. "What we're trying to do is build a sense of responsibility in people and empower them to do things."[52]

That's an important perspective, because authority to act has to be grounded in a clear understanding of shared vision, shared values, and trust. Authority, in this sense, springs from our level of knowledge maturity: the higher your maturity, the more cooperative you are and the more cooperation you inspire in others, because you understand the meaning of a shared identity and vision, and you're willing to act on that knowledge.

You aren't absenting yourself from the decision-making process—instead, you're investing your energy in building a sense of identity and collective purpose that *empowers* your team to act in ways that align with the bigger picture and the company's strategic goals and core values. In other words you're sharing the totality of your knowledge and helping your employees to use the totality of *their* knowledge, so that they can make faster and smarter interdependent decisions that benefit everyone.

7. Have the courage to act.

One key barrier to capitalizing on your knowledge is the fear of taking the action required to turn knowledge into action that leads to positive results. It's important to give people the authority to act, but you also need to help ensure that everyone—including you!—has the confidence and self-belief to turn ideas and possibilities into concrete action that drives real value.

It's surprisingly easy to fall into patterns of "learning paralysis" that make it hard to act on the things you know. As you surface and take stock of your own traits and weaknesses, it's important to look out for patterns of thought and behavior that impede action—not just hesitancy and self-doubt, but also issues such as perfectionism that make it harder for you to act decisively.

Often, such problems are tied up in our ego and our sense of who we are or who we wish we were. If I develop a big ego about my status as a book author, for instance, it becomes very easy to invest the book I'm writing with a kind of mythic significance that makes it almost impossible for me to put words on the page! It's only by accepting that the book I write *won't* be perfect—and that that's okay!—that I can find the courage and energy to keep on typing and eventually deliver a manuscript to my publisher. Knowledge is ever-evolving, after all, so any book I write will be a starting point, not the final word on the subject.

In much the same way, as leaders we need to work both to instill a kind of bias to action in ourselves and to identify those of our team members who struggle to turn ideas into action. We need to model the courage to strive for goals we aren't sure we can reach and ensure that our team as a whole understands that it's only by being tolerant of mistakes that we're able to forge a path to where we ultimately need to get to.

Often, this depends on recognizing that we're all on a shared journey, with a common mission and purpose, and that the challenges we face teach us things that will help us to keep moving forward. Seen in that light, the recognition and success of any one person is much less important than where we get to as a team. Spread that message, and your employees and colleagues will start to find a way to transcend ego (and the fear and paralysis it fosters!) and to work more decisively and courageously to execute strategies that drive benefits for everyone.

8. Find joy in the daily grind.

Every leader works hard, and leadership will never simply feel easy. But a knowledge-mindful leader tries to always find joy in that process—they bring their whole self to work each day, engage meaningfully and productively with everyone they meet, and capitalize on knowledge with deep purpose. That makes it much easier for them to avoid burnout: their leadership stops being a means to an end and becomes a rich and enriching experience—a true labor of love through which they are privileged to find their own best self and to help others become the best versions of themselves too.

Seen in this way, leadership becomes a privilege and a vocation—a natural outflowing of all the things that matter most to you as a human being. Work-life balance, in this sense, doesn't come from drawing lines separating "work" and "life." It comes from making your work and your leadership an *expression* of your life and a manifestation of the things that you value most and that encapsulate the totality of your self.

To put it another way, your work needs to become its own reward—and staying present in the moment is the only way to make that happen. Consider the hundreds of ramen shops that cluster together on some streets in Tokyo. Each one is busy selling noodles to passersby, and inside each one you'll find a chef who's busy making his ramen the absolute best it can be. There's no intention to franchise the restaurant or expand or take over other ramen joints—simply a commitment to the immediate task, the present moment, and the urgency of getting small details right.

The Japanese call this idea *kodawari*, or the pursuit of perfection in the present moment, and it's a powerful aspect of Knowledge Mindfulness. The neuroscientist Ken Mogi offers another compelling example from a court musician in Japan whose family had played at imperial palaces for over 1,300 years. Many of the musician's ceremonial concerts were in honor of obscure emperors and went completely unattended. "We play instruments, sing and dance, while no audience is present," the musician said. "We feel as if the spirits of the deceased emperors come down from heaven, stay for a while with us, enjoy the music, and then go back."[53]

> *Work-life balance doesn't come from drawing lines separating "work" and "life." It comes from making your work and your leadership an expression of your life.*

That sort of self-sustaining presence and joy is precisely what the knowledge-mindful leader should strive for. When you're fully aligned in the purpose and the mission and the big picture, it becomes possible to live more fully in each moment and to commit wholeheartedly (and with a higher level of knowledge maturity!) to each and every challenge or task or obstacle you confront.

9. Always think of the consequences.

The Iroquois people, whose ancestral lands included much of what is now upstate New York, believed that any decision should be considered in terms of how it would affect not just those now living, but all their descendants over the next seven generations. This idea of "seven-generation stewardship" is a powerful reminder that the things we do today affect a vast number of people, both living and not yet born, and also all the other living beings that are part of our ecosystem.

As knowledge-mindful leaders, we need to bring a similar kind of long-termism to our planning and decision-making. Most business leaders find that counterintuitive: we've gotten used to the idea that what matters are the daily stock-price performance, the monthly sales figures, or the quarterly profit-and-loss statement. We're wired to think in terms of short-term results—even when that mindset leaves us stuck on an obviously unsustainable path.

The reality, though, is that long-termism isn't *opposed* to short-term gains. It simply means recognizing that short-term gains only matter if they can be sustained over time. That often means sharing success with others: if you were to grab *all* the money in circulation, then money itself would become worthless. It's only by exchanging and trading and sharing that success—monetary or otherwise—becomes really meaningful.

A knowledge-mindful leader recognizes and remembers that. They don't feel bad about making a profit or coming out ahead in any given deal or negotiation, of course. But they understand that true success *only* comes when you build for the long term, and that means seeing yourself as a true steward of the ecosystem within which you operate.

10. Don't let success stop you.

As you elevate your personal wisdom and your collective insights, you'll find your understanding deepens and you gain a far richer sense of the possibilities and opportunities that exist for you and your team. It's important to remember, though, that success isn't an end point!

No matter how good things get, you can't simply rest on your laurels or close your eyes to the changing world around you.

This is something we see in the business world all the time, of course. There are plenty of companies that build one successful product but fail to pivot in new directions as the market evolves or new technologies and competing products are developed. The key, for organizations and individuals, is to see each success not as a final destination but rather as a stepping stone to the next challenge and the next opportunity.

Apple is a classic example, of course: Steve Jobs turned his computer and software empire into the launchpad for a wildly successful new category—the iPod!—then used that success, in turn, to pave the way for the iPhone, then the iPad, and now wearables like the Apple Watch. He saw each success not as the answer to a question, but rather as prompting *new* questions, revealing *new* things about his customers, and leading him on *new* journeys of exploration and innovation.

For knowledge-mindful leaders, our goal should be to cultivate a similar spirit of restless inquiry and ensure that our successes don't blind us to the things we *don't* yet know or understand. The goal—always, and perhaps especially when things are going well—should be to use the Three Cs Loop and continue the cycle of creating, connecting, and capitalizing, while also renewing, disconnecting, and acting on the things we've learned and discovered along the way.

This means being sensitive to the signals coming in from our customers and the world around us and the signals coming from within our organization. It might sound facile to say that we need to keep paying attention to what's going on around us, but the reality is that most successful business leaders grow isolated and removed from the communities they lead and serve. For knowledge-mindful leaders, that kind of insidious insularity is something we always have to watch for and guard against.

Finding a Deeper Purpose

When you bring together all three sides of the golden triangle in a continuous movement, you'll find you're able to elevate your knowledge maturity faster and faster—because the more you succeed in one area, the greater the impact you'll have in others too. After all, the reality is that the "three sides" of the triangle aren't discrete or separate—the reason they're so interconnected and interdependent is that they're aspects of a single unified thing, with growth in one area necessarily driving growth in others too.

Crucially, as your knowledge maturity increases, you don't just get better at doing the things you do. You also get better at deciding where to put your attention: what *should* you focus on? Which things should you do, and *how*, and *why*? In other words your escalating knowledge maturity helps you to find more meaningful ways of *using* your knowledge and to unlock a more meaningful purpose for yourself and those around you.

Knowledge maturity, after all, is in large part anchored in interdependence rather than independence and in the realization that *everything* is deeply connected. This interconnectedness, in fact, is what makes transformation possible: it's only by viewing things as part of a system that we enable change and growth across the system as a whole. That's why, as you continue to elevate your knowledge maturity, you'll find yourself looking for opportunities to have an impact that doesn't just benefit you, but that drives systemic and sustainable results for others, too, and opens up new possibilities and opportunities for everyone.

Of course, elevating your knowledge maturity takes time. Capitalizing on your knowledge will deliver ever-greater benefits along the way, but it isn't a single destination to be reached. There will always be more to learn and new levels of maturity to climb toward.

As you elevate your knowledge maturity, however, the reality within which you operate—your worldview—becomes clearer, and your perception will extend in both scope and height. You'll be able to see the interconnectedness not only between you as a leader and the people you lead and the actions you take, but also between your purpose and potential and the bigger picture of your life.

As you grasp this realization more fully, you'll find that it brings you joy and fulfillment in ways you've never previously experienced—and you'll find yourself committing and recommitting to this ongoing journey with an unprecedented energy and force.

Conclusion

Make Your Life Worth Living

I f you find yourself at a loose end on a Sunday morning, you could do worse than tuning in to *Sunday TODAY with Willie Geist*—and especially the "Life Well Lived" spot that each weekend celebrates the amazing lives of people who've recently passed away. From pioneering reporters to war heroes and civil rights attorneys to astronauts, the show pays tributes to people who've lived incredibly rich lives and who've enriched us all along the way.

Still, I find these segments perplexing, because they prompt a simple question: how do the show's producers *decide* whose lives were well lived—and do I agree with their decisions?

It's pretty clear that the show is designed to highlight people who made a big impact and whose lives were packed with significant tangible achievements in the world. That's great, of course—but were those people also *happy*? Did they live their lives in ways they found meaningful and rewarding, and were they fulfilled on a deep and enduring level?

When I'm old and wrinkly and look back on all I've done, I know I'll want to feel *my* life has been well lived—and I also know that my achievements are only one of the metrics I'll use to weigh my success. I do want to acquire and achieve certain things, of course. But I also want to feel that I've made my own life and other people's lives *richer* through the things I've done.

As I think about how to make my own life worth living, I know that I'd like to make a tangible impact. But I know that I'm also looking for other things: a sense of joy and satisfaction, a feeling of having loved and been loved, and a deep happiness—with fewer regrets and a faster path to maturity—that goes beyond simply cataloging the items on my resume.

In the previous chapters, I've tried to show that we have it within us to find a path forward that delivers just that: a series of opportunities—of interconnected windows—that we can use together to elevate the way we live and the way we conceive of and strive toward success. Even amid the chaos of the VUCA world, it's possible to step up and take control—to find a way to elevate your knowledge maturity, enrich your relationships with others, and open the door to a truly fulfilling and worthwhile life.

What Makes a Life Worth Living?

Finding that path forward starts with understanding that success isn't a single thing. One of the saddest things I've ever heard was oil tycoon H. L. Hunt's comment that money matters because it's the only way to keep score of how successful you are. Hunt achieved incredible things as a businessman, of course, but if he measured his success solely in terms of the number of zeros on his bank statement, then I'd say he missed out on leading a truly worthwhile life.

Now that you've read this book, I hope my reasons for saying that are clear. Money can help to make you happy, of course, but research shows that once you get to a certain level of financial stability, acquiring more money doesn't *add* anything to your total happiness and well-being. Success, then, can't just be about how rich you are, or how much stuff you have, or what title you have on your business card. Instead, it's something that emerges from the interconnected systems of which we're part.

That comprises many tangible things—wealth and promotions, yes, but also the concrete impact we have in our organizations, the growth we foster, and the changes we spark. And it also comprises many *intangibles*: the things we learn, the way we feed those learnings back into our self, and the feelings of satisfaction and fulfillment that arise from that cycle of personal growth and evolution.

Success doesn't lie in any one of those things. It's emergent from *all* those things and in the way we integrate them and find connections between them. Above all it's inherent in the way that these interconnections become more than the sum of their parts and give rise to a lived experience that's more enriching, satisfying, and joyful in every way.

Don't picture success as a fixed or static thing or as the stretched ribbon that you run through at the finish line. It's really something dynamic and changing: it's the journey, the growth, and the sense of deep fulfillment that comes from knowing you're getting better, evolving, and challenging yourself to reach higher and connect more deeply with yourself and those around you. Money and promotions are wonderful—but if you don't find these deeper connections and fulfill your potential, you're robbing yourself of the success you truly deserve.

Lessons from Knowledge-Mindful Leaders

Part of what I'm promising you in this book, of course, is that through Knowledge Mindfulness you can find your way to this kind of deep and rewarding success. The key insight I'm asking you to consider here is that joy and fulfillment aren't at odds with more traditional measures of success—instead, they make conventional success easier to achieve.

When you leverage the "golden triangle" and cycle through the windows of opportunity that it represents, you can access new ways to elevate your life and your leadership and to drive better results for yourself, your team, and your organization—and to have a positive impact that reaches many people, not just a few. The greater your knowledge maturity, the more you'll find pathways to deep, enduring, and multifaceted success!

> *Joy and fulfillment aren't at odds with more traditional measures of success—instead, they make conventional success easier to achieve.*

Think of it as a giant staircase with towering ten-foot steps. On your own you might be able to clamber up to the next step, and then the next, and gradually haul yourself higher. But when you connect with others, accepting a helping hand from those above you, and turning around to help others to ascend in turn, you'll find it exponentially easier to elevate yourself and your practices—and you'll create values and results for *everyone* and succeed in far bigger and more meaningful ways.

This is the secret sauce that makes Knowledge Mindfulness so profoundly important. Leaders who have high knowledge maturity are happier, of course. But they're also more effective, more inspired, and more empowered to drive meaningful change and spark powerful growth across their organizations—and to spark the same transformative, uplifting personal evolution and continuous growth in those around them.

In today's economic climate, when leaders are constantly being asked to do more with less, Knowledge Mindfulness offers a way to slice through the Gordian knot and unlock new efficiencies, new strategies, and new ways of creating value. By leading with compassion and humanity, it's possible to elevate knowledge maturity across your team and generate, share, and capitalize on knowledge far more effectively. Critically, when you also work to renew, disconnect, and continually act, you can drive growth and innovation without burning out your employees or driving yourself to the point of physical collapse.

Instead of treating your organization like a machine—running faster and faster, producing more and more—the knowledge-mindful leader understands the importance of addressing your organization as a collection of *people* with needs, values, insights, and knowledge that goes beyond simply the functional roles they play. Let's look at a few examples of knowledge-mindful leaders who I believe achieved this kind of success and ask what made them so successful:

Respond like "Sully" Sullenberger

When "Sully" Sullenberger's Airbus A320 struck a flock of geese one January morning in 2009, completely disabling the engines, the US

Airways pilot didn't panic. He followed the key rules every pilot knows by heart: aviate, then navigate, then communicate. Sully first made sure he had control of the plane—then he figured out where the nearest airport was, realized he wouldn't be able to reach it, and made the difficult decision to put his jetliner down in the Hudson River. Finally, he communicated clearly both with air traffic controllers and with his frightened passengers. The end result: a potential catastrophe was averted, and every single passenger survived the splashdown.

Even with years of training and experience as a fighter pilot, Sully found himself in a situation he could not have anticipated or prepared for. But because he was calm and composed, he was able to rapidly integrate new information into his perspective on the situation and make critical assessments with seemingly superhuman speed. Instead of trying to turn the plane around and head back to the airport—a decision that might have led to him crashing in a densely populated area—Sully found a creative, compassionate, and courageous solution that simultaneously saved his passengers and minimized the risk to others.

That's the power of Knowledge Mindfulness in action: the ability to respond to completely new and disconcerting situations, integrate your experience and training and novel information and core values, and bring all of that together to find solutions that drive better results for everyone. Because he was able to act with confidence and conviction, even amid terrifying uncertainty, Sully was able to save his plane, inspire others, and ensure panic didn't set in as the plane splashed down and was safely evacuated.

Find Joy like Richard Branson

Richard Branson is a great example of joy and creativity in action. He's known for leading with an infectious smile: whether he's running a music label or an airline or trying to pilot a hot-air balloon around the world single-handed, he brings the same energy and optimism to all his projects. Through sheer force of personal charisma, he inspires others to reach higher and tackle (and overcome) challenges they might never otherwise have taken on.

Not all of Branson's ideas work out, of course. (When was the last time you drank a Virgin Cola?) But precisely because he's full of ideas, Branson has the humility and confidence necessary to recognize when a strategy isn't working and rapidly pivot in new directions. Despondence and pessimism simply aren't part of his emotional repertoire, and as a result he inspires the organizations he leads to keep on fighting and finding new paths forward, even when times get tough.

Importantly, Branson's sense of joy doesn't just manifest in his trademark flashy grin. It's something he tries to spread across his organization, through the compassion, respect, and openness he brings to dealing with employees—and that he tries to draw out in others too. The best employees, he explains, are those who bring their whole self to work and who find value in engaging with other people's whole selves too. "I look for kindness," he explains. "I look for people who can bring out the best in others. They look for the best in others. They listen genuinely."[54] Now *that's* knowledge-mindful leadership.

Keep Learning like Ratan Tata

As one of India's richest men, industrialist Ratan Tata could be forgiven for taking a victory lap. Instead, he's earned a reputation as one of the most humble business leaders around: he flies economy, rides up front so he can chat to his driver, and makes a point of chatting to the people he meets. In Tata's eyes, everyone is equal: he might be a CEO, but there's still something to be learned from every person he meets.

That commitment to continuous learning is a hallmark of knowledge maturity, and it has defined Tata's career. When he was still a young man, he was offered a prestigious job at IBM—but turned it down and instead spent eight years in training roles on the shop floor at Tata Steel. And now that he's retired? He's been taking piano lessons. "If you want to be successful in life you should never stop learning," he explains.[55]

Tata's humility also shows in his philanthropy: he's given vast sums to support good causes, and it's telling that he's one of the world's biggest donors to educational institutions. Learning is a passion for Tata, and he's determined to facilitate learning in all its dimensions—whether it's by building innovation hubs for Ivy League universities or simply chatting to the person next to him on a long-haul flight.

Communicate like Oprah Winfrey

Oprah Winfrey is a tremendous communicator but also an incredibly smart businesswoman. In fact, of course, the two things go hand in hand: her gift for communicating and connecting with people *is* her business. Her publishing and broadcasting empire depends on her ability to both listen to others and to share knowledge with them in language that will resonate—a powerful cycle of empathy and continuous two-way feedback.

In fact Oprah says that it was only when she realized this that her career truly took off. The first few years of producing her talk show, she set out to create a successful talk show with lots of viewers—and, of course, she succeeded. But then, crucially, she *stopped* striving for tangible success and started reaching for intangible connections with others. "I stopped trying to do a show and told my producers we have only one intention and that is, how do we serve our audience and be a force of good in their lives?" she recalls—and it was *that* commitment that made her show a real cultural phenomenon.[56]

What's striking about Oprah is that she brings both self-awareness and emotional intelligence to her leadership. Whether she's interviewing royals or film stars or speaking to caterers or lowly interns, she tries to find a common spark of humanity, then fan that spark into a meaningful relationship. For Oprah *nothing* is simply a transaction: every connection is an opportunity to learn, connect, and grow. That, more than anything else, is what makes her a truly inspirational leader.

Lead the Way to Lasting Success

Each of these leaders has something different to teach us, of course. Knowledge Mindfulness manifests in different ways for each of them, because it's always deeply interconnected with the uniqueness of each leader and their circumstances.

But Knowledge Mindfulness also reminds us that we shouldn't simply try to emulate our heroes. There's only one Oprah and only one Richard Branson—and there's only one *you* too. The key to success is not just to learn from these amazing leaders, but to integrate those learnings into your *own* blend of knowledge and into your *own* leadership and as you figure out how to be the best you can possibly be.

Knowledge Mindfulness tells us that it's possible to capitalize on our knowledge in ways that do bring us tangible benefits but that *also* let us take a more joyful and positive and humane approach. Instead of obsessing about economic success, Knowledge Mindfulness offers us a way to achieve that success while *also* achieving personal, emotional, and spiritual success—and helping others to do the same. It also helps us to anticipate and recognize the consequences of our actions and our decisions, ensuring that we operate as a positive force—for people, for society, and for the world.

We can achieve that because as we strive to accelerate and elevate our knowledge maturity (instead of opting to stay in our comfort zone), we're increasing the quality of our knowledge by increasing the scope and depth of our understanding. That process also improves the quality of our perceptions of the world, the quality of our connections with others, and the quality of our actions and our decisions—so by elevating our knowledge maturity, we're able to unlock both tangible *and* intangible benefits for ourselves, others, and our organization as a whole.

The more you elevate your knowledge maturity, the more your life—both professional and personal—will gain depth and meaning. Your performance will improve, yes, but you'll also come to realize that happiness isn't some theoretical, faraway destination—it's something to be found in the day-to-day experience of your life. The most direct and immediate product of practicing Knowledge Mindfulness, in fact, is a more joyful, satisfying, and rewarding leadership experience.

We all know that the longer we live, the more we learn. But we shouldn't mistake learning for truly living! Learning is a way of adapting in order to survive—but it's when we go *beyond* just gobbling up information and start to embrace and elevate our knowledge that we find deeper meaning behind our lived experiences. Learning, at the end of the day, is individualistic and thus limited in its potential; knowing, on the other hand, is transformative precisely because it depends on recognizing and embracing the interconnectedness of ourselves and the world.

We live in an uncertain world, and to overcome the stress, anxiety, and fear—to not only survive, but also grow and thrive—we need to seek not just "know-how" but also "know-why" and find ways to mindfully build up our own unique knowledge. It's through *knowing*—knowing who we are, knowing others, knowing our place and direction and purpose—that we can find true fulfillment and success as leaders in a VUCA world. Better yet, the success we find won't be exclusively short-term or long-term success: it will be both, as we use our knowledge maturity to guide both our responses to immediate challenges and short-term goals and to the way we attend to long-term visions and aspirations.

Knowledge Mindfulness, in this sense, removes the pressures that come from external systems—be they economic, social, or political—and reforms their perspective and their practice to imagine new ways to live and to lead. Knowledge Mindfulness isn't esoteric or abstract—it's a practical way to reclaim your freedom and choose to grow beyond the challenges you face. Embrace this, and the lines between you and others, and between "us" and "them," will start to blur—these arbitrary distinctions will fade, and you'll find yourself able to live your own life far more vividly, passionately, and joyfully, both with others and for others.

Building Knowledge-Mindful Organizations

As you begin to integrate Knowledge Mindfulness into your life and leadership, and to understand the power and importance of elevating your knowledge maturity, you'll find that your growth and personal evolution transmit naturally to those around you. Elevating our knowledge maturity helps us to become less judgmental, more respectful, more engaged with the potential and possibilities that come from listening to and connecting with those around us.

As you forge links between the different elements of the golden triangle (personal wisdom, collective wisdom, and action) and create knowledge flow by using the Three Cs Loop to elevate your knowledge maturity, you'll find a transformation continuously taking place in both your own self-development and your impact on the external world. Over time this cycle becomes a way of life—call it "the art of knowing"—and also becomes something that you naturally share with others, inspiring those around you to emulate your behavior and follow your path to elevated knowledge maturity.

This is reinforced by the fact that through elevating our knowledge maturity, we create and recreate strategies and processes that are powered not just by immediate tactical needs, not even by strategic goals, but by deeper core values that define us and unify our organizations. Change resistance, the key obstacle to growth and value generation, here melts away—because the benefits you're fighting for don't accrue solely to you, but to everyone. People recognize that you aren't trying to extract value from them, but rather inviting them to rally together around a common goal.

This strengthening, self-reinforcing cycle of trust and interconnectedness helps to illustrate the fundamental truth that the growth of the individual and the growth of the organization are inextricably connected. Knowledge Mindfulness sets the stage to seek uniqueness not through separation but through deeper participation in the whole.

The more fertile an environment we create, the more we will grow and the more our organizations will grow too.

The tactics I've shared throughout this book are designed to help you achieve that in your own life—by generating the energy of the "golden triangle" of balanced and self-reinforcing Knowledge Mindfulness across your life, your leadership, and your organization. As we look to build organizations capable of rising to the challenges we now face, and as we look to sculpt ourselves into the kinds of leaders capable of inspiring success and supporting our teams, after all, it's clear that there's an urgent need to rethink the way we approach leadership, knowledge management, and organizational behavior.

Old ways of thinking about leadership, about knowledge, and about success are valuable in their own right. I'm not suggesting we throw them away! But we need to build bridges that connect these old approaches to the challenges we now face—and that starts with understanding and recognizing (or seeing clearly) the role that knowledge plays in our lives and in our organizations.

Through Knowledge Mindfulness, we can find ways to live and lead differently and in ways that are better suited to the VUCA world. The world is always changing, so we'll always need to keep finding new tactics and strategies—but by leveraging the Three Cs Loop, we can continuously and consciously generate and renew knowledge at the individual and collective levels and translate that knowledge into the action we need to drive more holistic success.

The Continuing Journey

I want to leave you with one thought that I hope you'll carry forward: remember, there is no end point or final destination. Knowledge

Mindfulness is a continuing journey: the more we capitalize and succeed, both individually and organizationally, the more important it becomes to keep going and finding ways to build richer lives for ourselves and others. This is what creates zest in our own lives and in the lives of others.

It's said that sharks have to keep swimming in order to keep water moving over their gills; if they stop moving forward, they'll die. Knowledge Mindfulness shows us the importance of continual forward momentum and knowledge evolution in our own lives too. Stagnation and isolation are dangerous; it's by continually connecting, interacting, integrating, and growing that we'll find our way through this VUCA world.

By now you should have realized that while Knowledge Mindfulness is incredibly powerful, it isn't a shortcut or a quick trick. Instead, it's an ongoing process—an ongoing practice—that works best when it becomes a true way of life. The more we put Knowledge Mindfulness at the heart of the way we live, the more it will manifest in our leadership, our decisions, our actions, and the way we impact both our organization and the people who depend on us.

> *Stagnation and isolation are dangerous; it's by continually connecting, interacting, integrating, and growing that we'll find our way through this VUCA world.*

Practicing Knowledge Mindfulness in this way—with commitment, creativity, integrity, and compassion—offers us the chance to unlock transformative success for both ourselves and others. Keep "knowing" into this process over the days, weeks, months, and years that lie ahead, and you'll find yourself driving positivity and powerful results for yourself, your team, and everyone whose life you touch.

Over time you'll find Knowledge Mindfulness becoming part of the warp and weave of your life. It will color and render vivid every moment of your day, helping you remain present in each moment and each interaction while also transcending ephemeral challenges and remaining anchored in the bigger picture—and broader ecosystem—of your life. Working consistently to elevate your knowledge maturity might not always be easy, but it *will* always be rewarding—and for today's leaders, it's the path to a life that truly *is* worth living.

Endnotes

1   Peter Drucker, *Management* (New York: HarperCollins, 1985), 514.

2   Peter Drucker, *Managing in a Time of Great Change* (New York: Routledge, 2011), 69.

3   Mark S. Granovetter, "The Strength of Weak Ties," *American Journal of Sociology* 78, no. 6 (1973): 1360–1380.

4   Katie Marriner, "America's Biggest Ports Handled a Record 50.5 Million Shipping Containers Last Year," *MarketWatch*, February 23, 2022, https://www.marketwatch.com/story/americas-biggest-ports-handled-a-record-50-5-million-shipping-containers-last-year-11645539342.

5   Carolyn Dewar, Scott Keller, and Vikram Malhotra, *CEO Excellence* (New York: Scribner, 2022), 3.

6   Yuval Noah Harari, "21 Lessons for the 21st Century | Talks at Google," YouTube, October 11, 2018, https://www.youtube.com/watch?v=Bw9P_ZXWDJU.

7   Sue Cantrell, Robin Jones, Michael Griffiths, and Julie Hiipakka, "The Skills-Based Organization: A New Operating Model for Work and the Workforce," *Deloitte Insights Magazine*, September 8, 2022, https://www2.deloitte.com/us/en/insights/topics/talent/organizational-skill-based-hiring.html.

8   Christine Comaford, "Got Inner Peace? 5 Ways to Get It NOW," *Forbes*, April 4, 2012, https://www.forbes.com/sites/christinecomaford/2012/04/04/got-inner-peace-5-ways-to-get-it-now/?sh=486d6b216672.

9   Selena Iarson, "Microsoft CEO Satya Nadella to Women: Don't Ask for a Raise, Trust Karma," *ReadWrite*, October 9, 2014, https://readwrite.com/nadella-women-dont-ask-for-raise/.

10   Jena McGregor, "19 Minutes with Microsoft's CEO: A New Book, a New Culture and a 'Complete Nonsense Answer'," *Washington Post*, September 17, 2017, https://www.washingtonpost.com/news/on-leadership/wp/2017/09/25/19-minutes-with-microsofts-satya-nadella-a-new-book-a-new-culture-and-a-complete-nonsense-answer/.

11   Ray Connolly, *Being Elvis: A Lonely Life* (New York: Liveright, 2017), 304, xix.

12   Hitendra Wadhwa, *Inner Mastery, Outer Impact: How Your Five Core Energies Hold the Key to Success* (New York: Hachette, 2022).

13   Roger Lipsey, *Gurdjieff Reconsidered: The Life, the Teachings, the Legacy* (Boulder: Shambhala, 2019), 60.

14   Humberto Maturana and Francisco J. Varela, *Autopoiesis and Cognition: The Realization of the Living* (Heidelberg: Springer Netherlands, 1980), 13.

15   Michael Polanyi, *The Tacit Dimension* (Gloucester, MA: Peter Smith, 1983), 4.

16   Gerd Gigerenzer, *Gut Feelings: The Intelligence of the Unconscious* (New York: Penguin, 2007), 19.

17   Antonio Damasio, *Descartes' Error: Emotion, Reason, and the Human Brain* (New York: Penguin, 2005), 188.

18 John Brockman, *Third Culture: Beyond the Scientific Revolution* (New York: Touchstone, 1996), 168.

19 Karl E. Weick, *Sensemaking in Organizations* (Thousand Oaks: SAGE Publications, 1995), 88.

20 Karl E. Weick, "Cosmos vs. Chaos: Sense and Nonsense in Electronic Contexts," in *Knowledge Management Tools*, ed. Rudy L. Ruggles III (Boston: Butterworth-Heineman, 1997), 253.

21 Matthew Polly, *Bruce Lee: A Life* (New York: Simon & Schuster, 2018), 285.

22 Donald Rumsfeld, *Known and Unknown: A Memoir* (New York: Penguin, 2011), 1.

23 Hans Christian Von Baeyer, *Information: The New Language of Science* (Cambridge, MA: Harvard University Press, 2004), 13.

24 Saint Augustine, *The Works of Saint Augustine: Vol. 1. The Confessions* (New York: New City Press, 2002), 491.

25 Kabir Edmund Helminski, *Living Presence: The Sufi Path to Mindfulness and the Essential Self* (New York: Penguin, 2017), 10.

26 Helminski, *Living Presence.*

27 Paul Hawken, *The Ecology of Commerce* (New York: HarperCollins, 1994), 1.

28 Ervin Laszlo, *The Self-Actualizing Cosmos: The Akasha Revolution in Science and Human Consciousness* (2014), 53.

29 Fritjof Capra, *The Tao of Physics An Exploration of the Parallels Between Modern Physics and Eastern Mysticism* (Boulder: Shambhala, 2010).

30 Jean M. Russell, *Thrivability* (Axminster: Triarchy Press, 2013).

31 The Dalai Lama, *Beyond Religion: Ethics for a Whole World* (Boston: Houghton Mifflin Harcourt, 2011), 21.

32 Daniel N. Stern, *The Present Moment in Psychotherapy and Everyday Life* (New York: W.W. Norton, 2010), 79.

33 Charles Darwin, *The Descent of Man, and Selection in Relation to Sex*, Vol. 1 (New York: D. Appleton, 1872), 79.

34 Laszlo, *Self-Actualizing Cosmos*.

35 Daniel Goleman, *Emotional Intelligence: Why It Can Matter More Than IQ* (New York: Random House, 2012).

36 John H. McDowell, *Mind and World* (Cambridge, MA: Harvard University Press, 1996), 42.

37 Frederick Winslow Taylor, *The Principles of Scientific Management* (New York: Harper & Bros., 1915).

38 Arie de Geus, *The Living Company: Growing, Learning and Longevity in Business* (London: Nicholas Brealey, 2011), 91.

39 Verna Allee, *The Future of Knowledge* (Amsterdam: Taylor & Francis, 2009), xiv.

40 John Donne, *Devotions upon Emergent Occasions* (Cambridge: Cambridge University Press, 1923), 98.

41 Nicholas Humphrey, *Sentience: The Invention of Consciousness* (Cambridge, MA: MIT Press, 2023).

42 de Geus, *Living Company*, 26.

43   Allee, *Future of Knowledge*, 4.

44   James Joyce, *Ulysses* (Oxford: OUP, 2008), 360.

45   Upton Sinclair, *The Brass Check: A Study of American Journalism* (Pasadena: Author, 1920), 349.

46   René Rohrbeck and Jan Oliver Schwarz, "The Value Contribution of Strategic Foresight: Insights from an Empirical Study of Large European Companies," *Technological Forecasting and Social Change* 80, no. 8 (2013): 1593–1606.

47   Richard P. Feynman, *Six Easy Pieces: Essentials of Physics Explained by Its Most Brilliant Teacher* (New York: Basic Books, 2011), xxii.

48   Kaomi Goetz, "How 3M Gave Everyone Days Off and Created an Innovation Dynamo," *Fast Company*, February 1, 2011, https://www.fastcompany.com/1663137/how-3m-gave-everyone-days-off-and-created-an-innovation-dynamo.

49   Bruce M. Boghosian, "Is Inequality Inevitable?", *Scientific American*, November 1 2019, https://www.scientificamerican.com/article/is-inequality-inevitable/.

50   Mike Landers, "Richard Montanez – Raza Report," *Lowrider*, June 14, 2011, https://www.motortrend.com/news/1108-lmrp-richard-montanez-raza-report/.

51   Howard Berkes, "Remembering Roger Boisjoly: He Tried to Stop Shuttle Challenger Launch," NPR, February 6, 2012, https://www.npr.org/sections/thetwo-way/2012/02/06/146490064/remembering-roger-boisjoly-he-tried-to-stop-shuttle-challenger-launch.

52   Anne Quito, "Netflix's CEO Says There Are Months When He Doesn't Have to Make a Single Decision," Quartz, April 19, 2018, https://qz.com/work/1254183/netflix-ceo-reed-hastings-expounds-on-the-netflix-culture-deck-at-ted-2018.

53 Ken Mogi, *Awakening Your Ikigai: How the Japanese Wake Up to Joy and Purpose Every Day* (New York: The Experiment, 2018), 106.

54 Abhijit Bhaduri, "Richard Branson: Decoding His Charisma," *The Times of India*, March 29, 2018, https://timesofindia.indiatimes.com/blogs/just-like-that/richard-branson-decoding-his-charisma.

55 Sthitaprajnya Panigrahi, "6 Leadership Lessons to Learn from Ratan Tata," *Consultants Review*, https://www.consultantsreview.com/news/6-leadership-lessons-to-learn-from-ratan-tata-nwid-2707.html.

56 Bill Murphy, Jr., "Oprah Winfrey Just Shared the Perfect Leadership Message for 2021. (It's Pure Emotional Intelligence)," June 13, 2021, https://www.inc.com/bill-murphy-jr/oprah-winfrey-just-shared-perfect-leadership-message-for-2021-its-pure-emotional-intelligence.html.

WEBSITE:

LailaMarouf.com

EMAIL:

Info@LailaMarouf.com

LINKEDIN:

www.linkedin.com/in/laila-marouf/